Contemporary Illustrations for Speakers & Teachers

A. Dudley Dennison, Jr.

Contemporary Illustrations for Speakers & Teachers

ZONDERVAN
PUBLISHING HOUSE OF THE ZONDERVAN CORPORATION
GRAND RAPIDS, MICHIGAN 49506

\

CONTEMPORARY ILLUSTRATIONS FOR SPEAKERS AND TEACHERS
Copyright © 1976 by The Zondervan Corporation
Grand Rapids, Michigan

Formerly published under the title *Windows, Ladders and Bridges*.

Library of Congress Cataloging in Publication Data
Main entry under title:

Contemporary illustrations for speakers & teachers.

  Published in 1976 under title: Windows, ladders, and bridges.
  1. Homiletical illustrations. I. Dennison, Alfred Dudley, 1914-
BV4225.2.W55   1979   251'.08   79-20651
ISBN 0-310-23631-2

Printed in the United States of America

To my beloved and talented wife, Ginny, whose contributions were monumental in the preparation of this book. No amount of marital persuasion, technique, or subtleness would entice her to accept co-authorship. The truly humble are so appealing, yet so inscrutable.

Preface

Lee Fisher, research associate for Dr. Billy Graham, recently mentioned to me in a letter "the illustration-starved ministers." This also applies to all people who do any amount of public speaking, whether secular or sacred. Coincident with Mr. Fisher's letter was one from Dr. Robert K. DeVries, Director of Publications for the Zondervan Publishing House. He had mentioned his doubts about the marketability of a series of radio messages I had given. Then he wrote this gracious and kindly statement: "Dudley, you are a master storyteller." He went on to suggest that I seriously consider a book of contemporary illustrations. Thus Ginny and I embarked on this project at once.

The world is a massive grab bag full of stories. Yet we become blinded to them as we voyage through the human predicament. But they are there, to be observed, recorded, and shared with our listening audience or faithful readers. As a physician I am constantly involved with the human scene and have a front-row seat on the joys and tears of life. These are to be shared, for they often carry a message or make a message sparkle.

We have scrupulously avoided any of the illustrations from my first three books, although many of the illustrations included in this book are based on my personal experiences. The published anecdotes have come from a variety of places. At times we were totally unable to determine the source. We had no difficulty finding a sufficient number of stories, and someday an encyclopedia of illustrations will be done by a sensitive writer. I am firmly convinced that the speaker, having difficulty in finding appropriate "windows" to light up his messages, will find his grab bag full, if he becomes an omnivorous reader, cleans his glasses, and each day observes the passing heartthrobs of life.

These illustrations are listed alphabetically by subject and where a story fits other categories as well, those categories are indicated in italic type at the beginning of the anecdote.

Index

Contemporary Illustrations for Speakers & Teachers

Advertising

A prominent West Coast newspaper woman, walking alone in New York City, chanced to see engraved on the cornerstone of a fashionable church the instructions Jesus gave His followers: "Heal the sick, cleanse the lepers, raise the dead, cast out devils." On an impulse, she walked around to the rectory door and asked to see the rector. "I saw your sign," she stated abruptly; and without further explanation she asked, "Do you?"

"Do I what?" asked the bewildered cleric.

"Do you heal the sick, cleanse the lepers, raise the dead, cast out devils?" Without waiting for the astonished minister to reply, she added, "If you don't, you shouldn't advertise."

Advertising

William Wrigley, the chewing gum magnate, who amassed a great fortune, attributed his success to advertising. While traveling on a train shortly before his death, he was asked by a friend why he continued to spend millions of dollars on advertising.

"Your gum is known the world over," argued the friend. "Why don't you save the millions you are spending on advertising?"

Wrigley thought a moment, then asked, "How fast is this train going?"

"About sixty miles an hour," replied the friend.

"Then why doesn't the railroad company remove the engine and let the train travel on its own momentum?" asked Wrigley.

Advice

Newsman Eric Severeid recalls a lesson he learned as a seventeen-year-old schoolboy. He and a pal set out to travel by canoe from Minneapolis to the historic fur-trading post of York Factory on Hudson Bay.

The last leg of the journey was the most difficult and dangerous. It lay across 450 miles of rugged wilderness with only one permanent settlement in the entire distance. The boys were awed by the prospect. But just as they were about to set out, an old fur trader gave them this advice:

"Just think about the next mile you have to go, not about the ones after that — never about all 450."

Mr. Severeid said that this advice had stayed with him through the years. "Many times in the future," he recalls, "I was to rediscover that there is only 1 mile to make, never 450."

Life

Age

Age is a quality of mind.
If you have left your dreams behind,
If hope is lost,
If you no longer look ahead,
If your ambition fires are dead,
Then you are old.

But if from life you take the best,
And if in life you keep the jest,
If love you hold,
No matter how the years go by,
No matter how the birthdays fly,
You are not old!

Aggressiveness

A speaker was delivering the commencement address. He was both colorful and dynamic as he kept hammering home to the graduating class point by point the importance of aggressive energy in attaining one's goal in life. Finally, in dramatic fashion he highlighted his point; thrusting his arm and forefinger out to his right, he thundered:

"What I am trying to tell you is that you're going to need an awful lot of what's written right there on the door!"

All eyes turned right as though at a given command, and there in bold black letters on the door was the single word *Pull*.

The speaker had forgotten which side of the door faced the assembly hall.

Agnosticism

An agnostic is a man who doesn't know whether there is a God or not, doesn't know whether he has a soul or not, doesn't know whether there is a future life or not, doesn't believe that anyone else knows any more about these matters than he does, and thinks it is a waste of time to find out.

James W. Dana

Alcohol

Until three years ago Jim was a hopeless drunk. His career, family, friends, and self-respect were gone before he was thirty. There had been more than thirty arrests in ten years, and desperate efforts to fight his way out of alcoholism had not produced any positive results.

He was on a bender in a small northern city when, once again, he was arrested by a foot patrolman. Hazily, he recalls struggling every step of the three blocks to the station house and getting in a couple of good swings at the arresting officer. The story would have ended here as in the past, and his life would have continued to deteriorate except for Officer McNeill.

Jim was released twenty-four hours after his arrest, and he headed down the main street toward the highway to hitch a ride out of town. He rounded a corner and came face to face with the same policeman who had collared him the night before. His bandaged nose attested that at least one of the wild drunken swings had connected. As he tried to blend into the atmosphere and slip past, the officer walked over and, using his first name, said, "How do you feel, Jim?" They spoke a few sentences to one another, then the officer said something Jim was never able to erase from his mind. He said, "Boy, oh boy, am I glad to see you tonight! You are a completely different man when you are sober, a completely different man."

The obviously heartfelt remark from one who had every reason to despise him, coupled with the obvious relief and concern etched in every line of Officer McNeill's face as he said it, caused something to snap inside Jim's brain. Nothing else said to him ever before had conveyed to him such a sense of dignity lost through his drinking. He stayed sober the next day and the following years to recoup a life lost in alcohol.

Alcohol

Nobody paid any attention to the shabby old man on San Francisco's Skid Row. He had been around for years, so long that he was taken for granted. He hobbled around on a cane, eked out a living with occasional odd jobs, and spent his earnings on cheap wine. For a long time he lived and drank alone in a shack behind a waterfront store. The bums who lived in the area knew only that his name was Al. Although they knew that Al preferred to be alone, they all liked him and even loaned him the price of a drink on occasion.

In the fall of 1959 they found Al's body beside an empty wine bottle. Cirrhosis of the liver, the coroner's report said. The few who had known Al over the twenty years he had drifted around the San Francisco slums prepared to forget another useless human derelict.

No one suspected that Al had been Lieutenant Alfred L. Beatie, graduate of the old Army Air Corps flying school at Kelly Field, Texas, and once one of the most promising flyers and officers in the nation. Among his classmates were many distinguished names.

Lieutenant Beatie proudly received his wings the same day as these men. He was a bright, handsome young man with a brilliant future. His classmates were all certain Al Beatie would have one of the most distinguished careers of the entire graduating class. No one suspected that Alfred Beatie, crippled in a crash shortly after graduation, would spend most of his life hobbling around Skid Row, forgetting his pain and loneliness in alcohol.

William P. Barker
Kings in Shirtsleeves

Alcohol

If alcoholism is a disease,
   it is the only disease that is bottled and sold; and it is the only
   disease that is contracted by the will of man;
   it is the only disease that requires a license to propagate it;
   it is the only disease that requires outlets to spread it.
If alcoholism is a disease,
   it is the only disease that produces revenue for the government; and it is the only disease that provokes crime;
   it is the only disease that is habit forming;
   it is the only disease that brings violent death on the highways;
   it is the only disease that is spread by advertising;
   and it is the only disease without a germ or virus cause.
It just might be that it's not a disease at all.

                                          Author unknown

Angels

We so often hear the expression "the voice of an angel!" that
I got to wondering what an angel would sound like. So I did
some research, and discovered that an angel's voice sounds
remarkably like a person saying, "Hurry up!"

Until the time I took over, research had been blocked be-

20

cause it was based on the delusion that the voice of an angel would always be beautiful. The words "Get up" are rarely beautiful, never less so than at 7 A.M. Yet that is always what the angels say when they are talking to men, as reported in the Bible. I can't think of anything an angel ever said but, "Get up and hurry!" An angel comes to Peter in jail and says, "Rise quickly." An angel says to Gideon, "Arise and go in this thy might." An angel says to Elijah, "Arise and eat." An angel appears to Joseph in a dream, when Herod is slaughtering the infants, and says, "Go quickly." An angel appears to Philip and says, "Arise and go."

Really, the angels are monotonous talkers! They always say the same thing — "Arise, hurry!" But so is a firebell monotonous. If we are to be saved, it will be by monotony, the reiterated command, "Get up and get going!"

Listen carefully and you can hear the voice of angels above the contemporary din of the world, a voice that ought to get us out of lounge chairs and comfortable beds. "Arise, go quickly!"

It might be a good idea to allow an angel to occupy the pulpit on Sunday. An irate hearer said to Samuel Barnett when he was canon of Bristol Cathedral in England, "I come to church to be comforted, and you sound like a fire alarm." Perhaps there was a fire.

Halford E. Lucock
in *Christian Century*

Accident

Anger

Dr. Leo Meadows, Professor of Psychiatry at the Medical College of Pennsylvania, noted the relationship between anger and accidents. An acquaintance told Dr. Meadows that he had had an accident, breaking his wrist and suffering a typical Colles fracture in a fall, but declared his accident was utterly unrelated to anger. "I simply went to answer the telephone, tripped over a chair, and fell on my hand which I had stretched out to break the fall."

The following details were ascertained. "It was a lovely day. I was working in the garden. My roses were coming up beautifully, and I was enjoying myself. I felt anything but angry. The telephone rang. My wife and daughter were inside, and I was sure they would answer it. It continued to ring and ring. I said, 'Oh . . . !' and went in to answer it." He began to laugh as it dawned on him what he had revealed — it was anger that had set him up for his accident.

Autograph

Applause

A little girl had been taken by her parents to hear a concert by a great pianist. As the artist was leaving the concert hall after giving a brilliant performance, the little girl walked up to him and asked politely, "May I please have your autograph?"

"No, dear," he answered somewhat curtly, "my hands are extremely tired from playing."

"And my hands are tired, too," she replied, "from applauding." She got the autograph.

Appreciation

Mother and father ran a store in the East for many years. One morning father answered the telephone and was heard to exclaim, "What! Picketing my store! What's come over them! They're my friends!" He rushed out of the house to the car. As he and mother drove to town, he asked, "Does anyone pay higher wages? Or give larger bonuses? Why, I pay them when they're sick and help with hospital bills. What's come over them?"

Just then they came in sight of the store. Sure enough, there was a large crowd in front and eight men were marching up and down carrying signs. It was mother who first realized the meaning of the scene. She read the signs aloud: "More Bosses Like Ours," "We Work Here and Love It," "You Can't Buy From a Nicer Guy."

Mother turned to dad, her face glowing. "They're wishing you a happy birthday, dear."

Author

A young woman interested in writing met author Joel Sayre at a party.

"Oh, Mr. Sayre, I wonder if you'd help me out?" she asked. "Tell me, how many words are there in a novel?"

The author was taken aback, but managed a sympathetic smile. "Well, that depends. A short novel would run about 65,000 words."

"You mean 65,000 words make a novel?"

"Yes," said Sayre, hesitatingly, "more or less."

"Well, how do you like that?" shouted the girl gleefully. "My book is finished!"

Advice

Author

A famous newspaper columnist received a large number of manuscripts from a young English writer asking his advice as to the best channel for marketing his writing.

He sent the manuscripts back with this note: "The one channel I can conscientiously recommend as the best outlet for articles of this type is the English Channel."

A.M.A. Journal

Age

Beatitudes

For the Aged

Blessed are they who understand my faltering steps and shaking hands;

Blessed are they who know that my ears must strain to catch the words they say;

Blessed are they who recognize that my eyes are dim, my wits slow;

Blessed are they who with cheery smile stop to chat;

Blessed are they who never comment, "You've told that story twice already";

24

Blessed are they who find ways to help recall pleasant days
    gone by;
Blessed are they who understand my loss of strength; and
Blessed are they who ease the days on my journey home in
    many loving ways.

Grit

Blessing

During World War I, a company of soldiers overseas received a shipment of Red Cross socks. Most of the boys had
holes in the socks they were wearing, and these new ones, which
had been knitted by the kind women of the Red Cross, were
certainly welcome.

The boys just barely had time to change to the new socks and
get on their leg wrappings when the order came to "fall in" and
start on a long march. No sooner had one boy taken a step than
a small hard object in the heel of his sock began to cause him
pain. Each step hurt more than the last one. But he could not
stop; the regiment was on the march. He gritted his teeth and
endured it, praying they would soon halt. Finally, when it
seemed he could not bear it another minute, there came that
welcome order to halt and fall out by the side of the road for a
few minutes rest. He sat down, unwrapped his leggings, unfas-
tened his hob-nailed boots, and jerked off the sock. He ran his
hand in it and brought out a little ball of paper that had been
rolled up very tightly. He unrolled it. There, in the uneven
writing of some dear, elderly soul, were the words, "God bless
your poor tired feet."

Josh Lee
How to Hold an Audience

Blessing

Dorothy Janvrin has been blind since the age of five as the result of an accident. She frequently traveled throughout the state lecturing to various organizations on what it is like to be blind. She says she never fully understood how well off she was until one evening when she was speaking to a group of young married couples. She told them she was a homemaker and the mother of four children. She also told them that she teaches piano, organ, and voice in her own home, to both sighted children and adults. She mentioned her many hobbies, such as crocheting, reading, writing, singing for weddings and funerals, tandem biking, swimming, and playing bridge.

When she finished her talk, a young mother of three children, a victim of polio three years earlier, wheeled herself up to Dorothy. Dorothy asked her much the same kind of things that she was accustomed to being asked. Did she do her own housework, ironing, cooking, and taking care of her children? Yes, she did all those things from her wheelchair. "My," the lady said to Dorothy, "I don't see how you do all the things you do, being blind like that."

"And I certainly don't see how you do all the things you do either," Dorothy answered.

Instantly there was a spark between the two — one of realization. Dorothy could sense, as her new acquaintance wheeled herself away, that she felt grateful that she had two good eyes. As for Dorothy, "Well, I suddenly realized all my rich blessings and was so grateful that I had two good legs to walk wherever I choose."

Blindness

When the blind lead the blind they do not always fall into the ditch. Take the life of Louis Braille, a blind French farm boy

26

who, by the time he was 18, had perfected the raised alphabet which bears his name.

Little is known of Louis' life except that he was plagued by ill health and ill fortune. But it is known that in 1812 at the age of 3, he was blinded while playing with an awl in his father's saddlemaking shop near Paris. France was in turmoil and nobody cared about the blind anyway; to most people they were beggars and thieves. What chance was there for little Louis?

But when he was 10, at a friend's urging, his father put him in an obscure school for blind children in Paris, where they used the regular alphabet, embossed so it could be read by the blind but not written. Louis studied music, but several times became discouraged and ran away, only to return because there was nothing in Paris for a blind child but ridicule and rough treatment.

When he was 14, death took his father, his mother, his best friend at school, and the devoted schoolmaster. But he plodded on, became an accomplished organist, and was made a teacher at the school.

He heard of a system of night writing used by the French army based on punching holes in cardboard. He spent three years developing this into his system; but when he demonstrated it before the Royal Academy, he was ignored. The new school director forbade him to teach it and for twenty years he tried to find support for his system; but gradually he succumbed to tuberculosis which took his life at the age of 43, in 1852.

But there is a sequel to the Braille story. In 1915, at the age of 55, the late William Hadley, a Latin teacher, lost his sight; but like Braille he refused to surrender. He studied Braille, and founded the Hadley Correspondence School for the Blind, which has given more blind people an education than any other organization in the world. Here is proof that the blind can and do lead the blind.

J. T. McCutcheon
in *Chicago Tribune*

Blindness

Several years ago in a school for blind children, a visiting clubwoman noted how half-heartedly the children saluted the flag. "They can't visualize it," the teacher explained. "To them it feels like just a piece of cloth." The woman took the problem to her club. "Let's make a flag the children can see with their fingers," she suggested.

The group got to work. Within a short time the flag was ready and taken to the school. The teacher spread it out on her desk and called a little boy up to her. As he traced the stripes, which were made of alternate strips of velvet and silk, she explained that these represented the thirteen original colonies. His fingers then ran over the felt field of blue to touch each star stitched in heavy silver thread, and his teacher helped him name the states of the Union. When he was done, he faced her with the glow of discovery on his face. "Now I know my flag," he said happily.

Boring

Once, at a senior class picnic, one girl accidentally dropped her graduation ring into the lake. Immediately, several of her male classmates volunteered to go diving for it. She said, "No, thank you," to her gallant companions then turned and asked her English professor to do it. Extremely flattered to be chosen over all those younger men, the professor dove into the lake. After several attempts he finally retrieved the ring. As he handed it to the girl, his masculine curiosity prompted him to ask her why she had chosen him over her younger companions to retrieve the ring. She replied, "Well, I have taken many of your courses, and I know that you can go down deeper and come up drier than any man I've ever known."

Politician

Career

A minister and his wife were worried about the future of their son. He was eighteen and showed no interest in anything. So they decided to put him to a test.

They put a Bible, a twenty-dollar bill, and a quart of whiskey on the table. If the boy chose the Bible, he would probably be a minister like his father. If he chose the money, he would be a banker or a businessman. If he took the whiskey, he would probably be a wastrel or a drunkard.

The parents called him into the room and asked him to make a choice. He looked over the temptations carefully. Finally, he stuck the twenty-dollar bill into his pocket, put the Bible under one arm, the bottle under the other, and left the room.

"Good heavens!" cried the minister. "He's going to be a politician!"

Nelson J. Lauth

Caring

Recently a patient came into my office accompanied by his minister. The reason: The man who had been totally deaf from birth needed someone who understood sign language to communicate his medical history to me. The clergyman carries on a ministry to the deaf of all ages in a large independent church in

Indianapolis, Indiana. He cares enough about one of his flock to spend two hours in a physician's office to communicate questions and answers. He cared enough to learn the sign language.

Chaplains

The American military chaplain corps, at least informally, can trace its history back to the Revolutionary War. Four clergymen were among the rebels who engaged the British at Concord Bridge on April 19, 1775. By the following June, when George Washington was appointed to command the Continental forces, fifteen ministers were voluntarily serving the spiritual needs of the army. Then, on July 29, 1775, the Continental Congress officially authorized chaplains for the army. This was followed on November 28, 1775, by the adoption of the second article of "Navy Regulations" in which Congress made provision for divine services afloat: "The commanders of the ships of the thirteen United Colonies are to take care that divine service be performed twice a day on board, and a sermon preached on Sundays, unless bad weather or other extraordinary accidents prevent."

Children

When her older sister was making plans to be married, twelve-year-old Peggy helped by running errands, answering the phone, and doing other jobs. But after the wedding when she saw the newspaper write-up, she said to her mother, "Boy, after all I did, I'm not even listed as one of the survivors."

Giving

Children

A visitor had left a quarter for seven-year-old Joey, and there was a discussion about what he should do with it. "Why don't you give it to the Red Cross?" suggested his older sister.

"I thought of that," said Joey carefully, "but I think I'll let the ice-cream man give it to the Red Cross."

Travel

Children

When the family returned from a four-thousand-mile trip last summer, the baby-sitter asked six-year-old Joanne what she thought of her vacation.

"Well," Joanne answered, "mostly we got up early and left."

Gratitude; Reward

Children

From the time she first learned to write, ten-year-old Celia had been encouraged to send personal thank-you notes for gifts received. It was only natural when a major chain-restaurant mailed her a birthday greeting and certificate for a complete dinner on the house that she laboriously penciled out her appreciation. Her mother tried to explain that this was not quite the same as a personal gift. "But somebody had to write it, and they're still people!" Celia insisted. "And they did send me a gift."

To our complete surprise, within a week a hand-written envelope with the official letterhead arrived from the company's main office in the East, addressed to Celia, personally. Eyes shining, she struggled to decipher the handwriting, which stated simply that the person writing was happy she would enjoy the outing; and he wished her the happiest of birthdays!

Her mother's cynicism was crushed and her confidence enhanced with just those few hand-composed sentences. She blessed that unknown executive somewhere, who, with just a few minutes of his time, quenched the idea that a large company is too big to care. If he could have seen Celia's radiant face as she said, "See, mom! They're just people, too!" he too would have felt well rewarded!

Parents; Punishment

Children

Little Bryan, who had just been punished, was silent and thoughtful over his lunch.

Finally, he looked up and asked his mother, "God can do anything He wants to, can't He?"

"Yes, dear," his mother replied. "God can do anything."

After a meaningful pause, Bryan looked up again and commented, "God doesn't have parents, does He?"

Show-and-Tell

Children

Five-year-old Jack was disturbed one Tuesday when he discovered his "show and tell" assignment was due in kindergarten class the following day. His grandmother and grandfather had been visiting and he had completely forgotten to find something of interest.

As the visitors planned their trip home Wednesday morning, a happy thought struck young Jack. He asked grandpa and grandma if they would stop at school on the way to the airport and say good-by. Naturally they complied. But when they entered the classroom, to their astonishment and the teacher's amusement, Jack turned to the class and said, "I have the best show-and-tell of all. Here are my grandparents, all the way from Florida."

Persistence

Children

She had just put her young son to bed for the umpteenth time, and her patience was worn thin. At last when she heard him cry "Mama" again, she yelled up at him, "If you call 'mama' one more time, I'll have to spank you!" After that there was silence. Then, just as she sat down for a minute of rest, she heard a wee whisper, "Mrs. Green, may I have a drink?"

Christ

You touched my world
Ever so gently
And brought life
To the infinity
Of every half-moment.
The morning sun
Of every tomorrow
Appeared
Over the mountaintop
Of my yesterday-heart
And the desert valley below
Sprouted
With the freshness of rain
And the warmth of noon.

You touched my world
Ever so gently
And the seed of love
Was planted.

Albert Haase
Unsharpened Pencil

Love; Race Relations

Christianity

The Clarks were the first black family to move into an all-white neighborhood. Before moving they made an inspec-

34

tion trip to their property. They saw a few of their future neighbors, but none of them spoke, and their indirect glances were less than friendly.

With doubt in their hearts they moved on a Saturday. They arrived before the moving van and began to unload the car. Almost immediately a teen-ager appeared from next door. "Hi, I'm Ted Davis," he said. "Welcome to our neighborhood. Here, let me help." Not waiting for an answer, he picked up two heavy boxes.

Not long after, his mother came to the door with a pot of coffee, some cold drinks, and doughnuts on a tray. In the center of the tray was a vase with two lovely red roses.

"Welcome," she said. "I'm Cora Davis, your corner neighbor. I didn't know if your utilities had been turned on, and I thought a cup of coffee might get you off to a better start."

Later the youngest Davis teen-ager came over and introduced herself. "Hi, I'm Donna Davis. Mother said I should bring your little ones over to our house. Moving is bad enough without children under your feet."

Their friendship has continued to grow. No matter where they go, they will never forget that mother and her children who acted out of Christian love instead of just talking about it.

Giving

Christianity

No great spiritual blessing ever comes to one who gives selfishly and grudgingly. A man was complaining to his pastor about the church's asking for money. He fumed, "This business of Christianity is just one continuous give, give, give." The preacher thought for a moment and then replied, "I want to thank you for one of the best definitions of Christianity I have ever heard."

Christianity

One bright autumn Saturday Celia stopped for lunch at a northside Chicago restaurant. As she sat down she was attracted to a young woman in the booth behind her. She wore a radiant, excited expression on her face and a bright corsage on her dress. Celia overheard the waitress say to the girl, "This is terribly exciting. Haven't you any idea who sent you the flowers?"

"No," the girl replied, "but I am so thrilled! I couldn't believe it last night when the doorbell rang and the flowers were delivered."

"Wasn't there a card?" the waitress asked.

"Yes, it said, 'Happy birthday from someone who cares.' And when this corsage came this morning it had the same message."

"I would like to do something for your birthday too," the waitress said, and she picked up the girl's check. As she left to serve another customer she called back, "Happy birthday!" The girl was smiling broadly when she left a few minutes later. Celia observed then that she was a hunchback.

Moved by this scene Celia asked the waitress about the little hunchback. She was told that the girl had no family or friends and led a lonely life. She had sent the bouquet of flowers and the corsage to the girl hoping to bring a little excitement into her life.

The waitress added that she was going to the hospital soon herself for foot surgery, and the doctors did not think she would be able to continue doing waitress duty. This was very disconcerting to her since she was the sole support of her two small children. But she wasn't discouraged. "After seeing the glow on that girl's face today, I am no longer afraid. I know that God will provide for my children and me."

Christianity

After the first World War there was an attempt to fly an expedition from Italy to the North Pole. This venture met with disaster somewhere in the cold northland. Back through Leningrad came the report that two survivors had been abandoned when they were unable to keep up through the Arctic cold. There was a great outcry in Russia at the inhumanity of leaving a friend to die in the snow.

At the same time, an American church was distributing food supplies to starving Russian peasants. One of the Soviets said to a representative of the American church, "Why would you come over here and bring food to us?"

The Russians could understand why one would not want to desert a dying friend in the snow but not why there were those who would come halfway around the world to be merciful and helpful to those who were dying of hunger. Helping a friend is common decency. Mercy and helpfulness toward those who are far away or those who are not especially friendly is Christianity.

Honor System

College

A student government officer at the University of San Francisco wrote the University of California concerning the use of the honor system during exams and received this reply: "The University of California abandoned the honor system several years ago when it became evident that the professors had the honor and the students had the system."

Dick Friedlich
San Francisco Chronicle

Athletics

College

A Chinese student attending one of our colleges was writing back to China and telling his friends and relatives about America and its institutions.

He defined an American university as follows: "An American university is a vast athletic association, where, however, some studies are maintained for the benefit of the feeble-bodied!"

*Football; Athletics;
Second Chance*

Comeback

On New Year's Day, in 1930, Georgia Tech played Southern California in the Rose Bowl. In that game a man named Roy Riegels recovered a fumble for Southern California. Somehow, he became mixed up and started running in the wrong direction. One of his teammates outdistanced him and downed him just before he scored for the opposing team. Tech took over the ball and scored, and that touchdown was the margin of victory.

That strange play came in the first half, and everyone watching the game was asking the same question: "What will Coach Nibbs Price do with Roy Riegels in the second half?" The men filed off the field and went into the dressing room. They sat down on the benches and on the floor — all but Riegels. He put his blanket around his shoulders, sat down in a corner, put his face in his hands, and cried like a baby.

If you have played football, you know that the coach usually has a great deal to say to his team during half time. That day Coach Price was quiet. No doubt he was trying to decide what to do with Riegels. Then the timekeeper came in and announced there were three minutes before playing time. Coach Price looked at the team and said simply, "The same men who played the first half will start the second." The players got up and started out — all but Riegels. He did not budge. The coach looked back and called to him again; he still didn't move. Coach Price went over to where Riegels sat and said, "Roy, didn't you hear me? The same men who played the first half will start the second."

Roy looked up and his cheeks were wet with a strong man's tears. "Coach," he said, "I can't do it. I've ruined you; I've ruined Southern California; I've ruined myself. I couldn't face that crowd in the stadium to save my life."

The coach reached out and put his hand on Riegel's shoulder, "Roy, get up and go on back; the game is only half over." And Roy Riegels went back, and the men on the Tech team will tell you that they have never seen a man play football like Riegels did that second half.

Commitment

A skinny Pentecostal country preacher from Pennsylvania felt called of God to minister in the worst slums of New York City. He stood on the corner of the most crime-ridden section of Brooklyn, an area designated as Fort Greene. There, the "Cross and the switchblade" met, as this insignificant, skinny country preacher told drug-ridden, sex-torn teen-agers that God loved them. "I told them that God loved them as they were, right then." He knew what they were. He knew their hatred and anger. He knew that some of them had committed murder. But God also saw what they were going to be in the future, not only what they had been in the past. Radical love! God's love! This young Pentecostal had nothing going for him humanly, but he had the Holy Spirit and love. In the end he brought Christ to a barren, pagan section of our society. How many of us love that way?

Helen Keller; Blindness;
Deafness; Teacher

Communication

A century ago, a young teacher in Alabama held her little blind-and-deaf pupil's hand under the stream of water flowing from a pump spout and manually spelled out the word *water*. The teacher's name was Anne Sullivan; the little girl's, Helen Keller. As a surprise for Miss Keller, her classmates at Radcliffe College presented a lovely fountain to the college on their fiftieth class reunion. The fountain is called the Anne Sullivan Memorial Fountain. Before feeling the water, Miss Keller read a Braille inscription on the back of the fountain: "In memory of Anne Sullivan, teacher extraordinary, who beginning with the word water opened to the girl Helen Keller the world of sight and sound through touch."

Eisenhower; Listening

Communication

The technique of listening is even more important in a democracy than in a dictatorship. Norman Rockwell, the noted artist, recounted his experiences while painting the portrait of President Eisenhower.

"The general and I didn't discuss politics or the campaign. Mostly we talked about painting and fishing. But what I remember most about the hour and a half I spent with him was the way he gave me all his attention. He was listening to me and talking to me just as if he hadn't a care in the world, hadn't been through the trials of a political convention, wasn't on the brink of a presidential campaign."

It was small wonder Eisenhower was such an effective wartime and civilian leader.

Applause;
Translation; Doctors

Communication

A Houston cardiologist delivered a paper at a medical convention in Mexico City and received only sporadic applause. The next speaker who got up spoke in Spanish. The audience constantly interrupted him with applause, and the Houston doctor joined in enthusiastically. Finally, a surgeon whispered to the Houston physician, "I wouldn't applaud so much if I were you. He is merely translating your speech."

Communication

Mike Ovikian, like any newcomer, took awhile learning American slang. While visiting a few days in a Minneapolis home, he teasingly told the housewife about some of the strange Middle East customs, which the lady could not believe. The next day the husband, tall and big, came to Mike and said, "Say, my wife tells me you were pulling her leg yesterday."

With a worried look Mike answered, "Oh, no, sir, I would never do such a thing to your wife."

Lee Fisher
*A Funny Thing Happened
on the Way to the Crusade*

Communism

Ronald Reagan, former governor of California, tells how we could match Russia's record after its more than half a century of socialism:

"We'd have to cut our paychecks back by more than 80 percent; move thirty-three million workers back to the farm; destroy fifty-nine million television sets; tear up fourteen of every fifteen miles of highway; junk nineteen of every twenty cars; tear up two-thirds of our railroad track; knock down 70 percent of our houses; and rip out nine of every ten telephones. Then all we have to do is find a capitalist country to sell us wheat on credit to keep us from starving."

Compassion

A group of college professors at a certain university were in the habit of meeting to consider any acts of misconduct on the part of the students. One afternoon they were talking about the bad conduct of one of the students and one professor insisted on severe punishment for the lad saying, "After all, God has given us eyes."

"Yes," replied one of his colleagues with a much more compassionate nature, "and eyelids, as well."

Love; Nurse

Compassion

Hulda was a petite, blonde, blue-eyed Swedish girl who was a nurse in a western state mental hospital. Very devout, she never missed a service of worship. Often she would drop into the prayer chapel of her church during the noon hour to spend a few moments in quiet thoughtfulness and prayer. One Sunday morning as she sat in worship her pastor was shocked to notice that her face was all cut, bruised, and scratched. He supposed she had been involved in an accident. When she went out the door and shook hands with him, he noted that her hands were covered with scratches and red marks. Not wishing to pry, since she offered no explanation, he did not probe. The last person out of church that day was the head nurse of the section in which Hulda worked. "What on earth happened to Hulda?" he asked her.

The head nurse told him, "Two weeks ago a fourteen-year-old girl was brought into the hospital, violently insane. A day later the psychiatrist in charge of that section told her story at the daily staff meeting. The little girl had been reared in abject poverty. Her mother and father were both alcoholics, and never in her entire life had she heard a single word of love. Never had she known what kindness and affection were, and never had she been made to feel needed or wanted. One day at age twelve she had watched her father and mother in a violent argument struggling for the possession of a shotgun. She had seen that shotgun explode and watched as her father's life ended on the floor. The mother, charged with manslaughter, was paroled, presumably to care for the child. But the next two years all she knew from her mother were curses and beatings. Her little mind became so filled with hatred and resentment toward all human beings, it rejected reality and snapped. Drifting off into fantasy and delusion, she became violently insane."

The physician told the staff that part of her therapy must be catharsis. She must be allowed to vent her wrath on someone, to spew out her pent-up hatred which had so poisoned her.

For one hour a day for two weeks Hulda had gone into the cell of this demented girl, allowing her to have her catharsis. Hulda took all the kicks, pounding, clawing, and scratching until, spent, the girl crouched in a corner, trembling like a frightened, trapped animal. Each day as Hulda left the cell she would pause, turn and face the girl, and with blood streaming down her face would smile and repeat these words, "Darling, I love you! Darling, I love you!"

This is like Christ! You are ingrafted in Christ. Fresh and new. What you do for others you do for Christ!

Surgery

Compassion

The Pharmaceutical Manufacturers' Association has sharply drawn the medical profession's attention to the impersonalism of the operating room. They emphasize the critical importance of physicians' keeping in mind that lying on the operating table is a person who is a living, breathing, suffering, and hearing human being. It has stressed the emotional content of all words spoken in surgery.

As the anesthetic is being given for major surgery, the patient panics when he hears somebody close by softly singing, "Nearer My God to Thee." Or, deadly fear may strike when the prone patient hears, "I'm going to shoot him now," or "Hook up the monitor" (to the drugged patient "monitor" sounds more like "monster"). Or, a doctor declares in disgust, "This just isn't my day." The frightened patient awake under spinal anesthetic frantically wonders what is wrong.

People are not to be disregarded or treated as cases or things without feelings or emotional responses.

Second Chance; Nurses

Compassion

In a lowly spot in England a young doctor was assigned to be in charge of a hospital. Later he was to become a famous author in his own right, but first he was to gather life experience. He had been there just a short time when a six-year-old boy was brought in with a severe case of diphtheria. The boy was gasping and choking and his life would be gone in a matter of moments unless emergency surgery was performed immediately. Even though he had never done the needed operation himself, the young doctor knew that only a tracheostomy would save the young life, so he made the incision into his windpipe. His assistant was a young nurse who had received her degree only a short time before. It seemed the job would never end, but at last the operation was completed. He inserted the tube into the incision allowing the lad to begin life-saving breathing once again.

In the early hours of the morning he heard a loud pounding on his door. When he opened it, there stood the young nurse who had assisted him. She had been assigned to sit up through the night to make sure the breathing airway stayed open. But though her spirit was willing, she was so exhausted from the strain of the surgery she had fallen asleep. While she slept, the tube had become blocked, and the boy had died.

The doctor lost his head and swore that she would have to pay for her mistake and he would report her gross negligence. He called her into his office and read the report he'd written while she stood trembling with fear and overcome with remorse and shame. When he had finished, he asked, "Have you anything to say?" Fearfully she nodded her head, dared to look up, turned her tear-stained face to him, and said falteringly, "Please, sir, give me another chance."

It had not occurred to the doctor that he might do this. Her mistake had cost a life. She must pay. It was that simple. But that night he couldn't sleep. He kept hearing her plea, "Please give me another chance." All night he wrestled, and the Lord tormented him with reminders of mercy and compassion. The next morning he tore up the report.

The young nurse went on to become head of a great children's hospital, loved by all; giving herself over and over to children who needed her love and great heart. Suppose the girl had fled and not faced the consequence of her wrong action? Suppose the young doctor had not given her another chance?

Would God do any less than he? He is a God of the second chance. That is why He exchanges prodigal's rags for robes of riches. Because He is a God of beginning again.

Concern

People say that Chicago is a cold, unfriendly city, but Melinda Smith knows differently. When her mother fell and broke her hip, and it was necessary to operate, she needed many pints of blood. The hospital asked the family to replace it if possible. Asking her friends to donate blood wasn't easy, and she worried what to do. Then one day the doorman of the apartment house where they lived handed her an envelope. As she read the letter inside, tears came to her eyes. The message said: "We would be happy to donate blood for your mother." It was signed by the elevator operators, maintenance crew, many of the tenants, plus the neighborhood butcher, baker, tailor, and druggist.

Concern

Rod was in his early forties when I first met him. He is a PhD and an ordained minister who was doing a magnificent job in a church-related field. I learned that one compassionate teacher's interest and concern had completely altered the entire course of this valuable man's life.

At a young age, it had been decided by his teachers, in consultation with his principal, that Rod was mentally retarded. His parents had been informed that soon he would be placed in another school where he would "fit in better" with other mentally retarded children.

The day before the proposed transfer, one of Rod's teachers took a few minutes to talk to the boy. The frightened lad opened up to this warm, friendly man. The teacher then announced to

47

the principal that Rod was not mentally retarded, just extremely frightened. An abusive father had made him absolutely petrified of all authority figures, rendering him mute in their presence.

What part does chance play in our lives? Where does our genetic wiring fit in, our programming by parents and others during our formative years? Not every frightened, noncommunicative child can be guaranteed the appearance of an earnest, compassionate, interested man at the crucial moment.

Confidence

Once, at a scientific gathering, a young physicist approached British astronomer Sir Arthur Eddington and asked: "Is it true, Sir Arthur, that you are one of only three men in the world who understand Einstein's Theory of Relativity?"

Then, noting the look of discomfort that came over the astronomer's face, he apologized. "I'm sorry," he said. "I didn't mean to embarrass you. I know how modest you are."

"Not at all," said Eddington. "I was just wondering who the third man could be."

E. E. Edgar
in *Coronet*

Conscience

A certain speaker was lecturing to a group of junior high students on the subject of conscience. He endeavored to illustrate his subject by telling how he went hunting with his bird dog. The dog ran here and there through the brush and finally stopped. With one foot lifted, he looked with intensity at a certain spot. They went toward that spot, and soon a convey of quail flew up. The hunter shot his quail.

The speaker then asked the question: "How did the dog know those quail were there?" He started to answer his own question, when a small boy shouted: "The dog had brains." When the students became quiet, the speaker explained that they all had brains but would not have known the quail were there.

He then went on to say that it took more than brains to sense the presence of quail. God gave the dog a special instinct that, when trained properly, could point out to a hunter just where the quail were located. Likewise, God has given to us, His children, an instinct called conscience that will help us to tell the difference between right and wrong when it is trained in the ways of the Lord.

First of all, develop your conscience by studying the life and teachings of Christ, letting His mind speak to your mind. "Let this mind be in you, which was also in Christ Jesus" (Philippians 2:5 KJV).

Faith; Sleep

Conversation

An aged woman who had seen much trouble but never complained was much beloved in her community. One day her pastor stopped to see how she was getting along. "Do you have any trouble sleeping?" he inquired.

"Not much," she answered.

"I suppose you just close your eyes and count sheep until sleep comes," the pastor suggested.

"No," was the reply, "I just close my eyes and talk to the Shepherd."

Conversion

The turning point in the life of Gert Behanna, the author of *The Late Liz,* began when she was invited by a wealthy friend in Connecticut to meet some people of her own social set who had had a vital experience of God. She had never met such people before, and got thoroughly drunk in preparation for the ordeal. As the dinner party progressed, Gert found herself chattering about all the unfair and unjust things that had been happening to her. Tom and Blanche Page listened quietly. Finally Tom said, "Gert, you certainly have a lot of problems. Why don't you turn them all over to God?" Gert was shocked and asked, "Do you mean like turning my luggage over to a redcap?" "Exactly!" Tom replied. Some days later, back in her Illinois home, Gert Behanna got on her knees and did just that. It was the beginning of a remarkable conversion.

Bruce Larson
Setting Men Free

Conversion

Several years ago Leighton Ford was conducting a crusade in Fredricton, New Brunswick. The Chevrolet dealer, a man with an evangelistic spirit, put a large sign on the front of his business. The huge letters said, "SUPPORT FORD." Underneath in small letters it said, "Support Leighton Ford Crusade."

Addressing a civic club, Leighton quipped, "When Chevrolet supports Ford, that's real conversion."

Lee Fisher

Cop-out

Linebacker Chip Oliver of the Oakland Raiders quit professional football to join a hippie commune. He does not intend to return to his $25,000-a-year job with the professionals. Those who visit Oliver find him drinking fresh carrot juice in a northern California collective. He has grown a shaggy beard and long hair. He talks about his membership in the One World Family of the Messiah's World Crusade.

After his last season as a pro, Oliver became a vegetarian and dropped in weight from 230 to 180 pounds. His first act upon moving into the commune was to give $5000 to a fifty-four-year-old man they call "the messiah."

This famous linebacker says he no longer wants to keep society's pace. His desire is to "cop-out, cut the cord, and start a new life." Chip felt it easier to say, "I quit," than to keep fighting.

Courage

You may remember A. J. Cronin's popular novel, *The Keys of the Kingdom*. One of the main characters in his book is Father Chisolm, a missionary priest who has worked almost all his life in China against overwhelming odds. In one passage this good Christian missionary gives a clue to his remarkable courage and hope. He is talking to a distressed friend, a native farmer, who is wringing his hands together and bitterly complaining because his garden has been completely washed out by a seasonal flood. "My plantings are all lost," he cries. "We shall have to begin all over again." Father Chisolm quietly replies, "But that's life, my friend: to begin again when everything is lost."

War; Lying; Hitler

Cover-up

When the drone of planes sounded over Germany's ancient town of Freiburg the night of May 10, 1940, scarcely a burger looked up. They knew their city was of no military significance.

Suddenly bombs whistled down. Freiburg's picturesque "old city" was heavily damaged. The next day Adolph Hitler screamed, "The allies violated an agreement to spare open cities." He vowed, "Five German bombs will fall for every enemy bomb," and then he tried to live up to it.

Nazi planes wiped out Rotterdam, swept across the channel, pulverized Dover and Portsmouth, and left London's inner city and the Cathedral of Coventry in flaming rubble. The words *blitz* and *total war* were added to the military language.

After prolonged insistence by the Western Allies who said none of their planes were near Freiburg that fateful night, the truth emerged. German officials, digging into the archives of the Institute for Current History at Munich, found that the bombers that hit Freiburg that night were German. Field Marshall Herrmann Goering had ordered them from Landsberg for a raid on Dijon, France. Lost in heavy clouds, Goering's bombers had dumped their load on Freiburg by mistake. Goering and Hitler agreed to cover up the facts and used the incident to justify the ruthless Nazi invasion of the Low Countries.

Death

A few years ago, a news photographer won an award for a

picture of "death" he had taken. A young woman was found dead in a sports car where she had died from an overdose of narcotics. Using a wide-angle lens, the cameraman had produced a picture showing not only the body pitifully sprawled across the front seat of the car but also the parking meter which read, "TIME EXPIRED."

D

Heart; Life

Death

Elena Frings, a young woman in her twenties, was informed by her doctor that her heart was so weak she had only six months to live. She decided to leave her office in Santiago, Chile, and work as a volunteer community organizer among the city's slum dwellers.

"That way I will die happy," she told a friend.

Miss Frings worked so effectively that she was invited to New York to give talks about the program. There, she met a surgeon who successfully operated on her defective heart.

Elena Frings is now back in South America, helping the poor who live on the fringes of life. It was her expectation of death — not the operation — that gave new direction and meaning to her life. "For where your treasure is, there will your heart be also" (Matthew 6:21 KJV).

Children

Death

"The more parents avoid the topic of death," writes Father P. J. O'Doherty, "the more their children fear it."

"The simplest way to introduce a child to a discussion of death," says Father O'Doherty, "is to talk about how flowers

53

and pets die. Emphasize the beauty and transience of life rather than the morbid details of death. Children need to be told that there is nothing wrong with crying and, above all, that the child is in no way responsible for the death of the person. It is important," he cautions, "to proceed slowly, step by step, according to the understanding of the child and the personal belief of the parents."

"Unless a grain of wheat falls into the earth and dies, it remains alone; but if it dies, it bears much fruit" (John 12:24).

Funeral

Death

One man recorded a talk to be played at his own funeral:
"This body which you now see and which has been the dwelling place of my spirit, will turn into dust. But when the time of the resurrection of my body comes, the same dust will again become the dwelling place of my spirit."

Death

Dr. Elizabeth Kubler-Ross, a psychiatrist and authority in the field of death dying, stated in a speech in Richmond, Indiana, that her research has convinced her that life continues after death. Her research has led her into the study of out-of-body phenomena. "Only the body dies," she told the conference on Interdisciplinary Ministry on Death, Dying, and Living at the Quaker Yokefellow Institute.

Recently she told an interviewer that she no longer believes, as she once did, that death is the end of everything. "Now I'm certain it is not," she concludes after studying reports on the experiences of the dying.

Decision

Slavery
1857

Abortion
1975

Although he may have a heart and a brain, and he may be a human life biologically, a slave is not a legal person. The Dred Scott Decision by the U. S. Supreme Court has made that clear.

A black man only becomes a legal person when he is set free. Before that time, we should not concern ourselves about him. He has no legal rights.

If you think that slavery is wrong, then nobody is forcing you to be a slaveowner. But don't impose your morality on somebody else!

A man has the right to do what he wants with his own property.

Isn't slavery really something merciful? After all, every black man has a right to be protected. Isn't it better never to be set free than to be sent unprepared and ill-equipped into a cruel world? (Spoken by someone already free.)

Although he may have a heart and a brain, and he may be a human life biologically, a fetus is not a legal person. The Roe vs. Wade decision by the U. S. Supreme Court has made that clear.

A baby only becomes a legal person when he is born. Before that time, we should not concern ourselves about him. He has no legal rights.

If you think abortion is wrong, then nobody is forcing you to have one. But don't impose your morality on somebody else!

A woman has the right to do what she wants with her own body.

Isn't abortion really something merciful? After all, every baby has a right to be wanted. Isn't it better never to be born than to be sent alone and unloved into a cruel world? (Spoken by someone already born.)

Decision

In his book, *A Life Worth Living*, C. A. Roberts tells of meeting W. C. Coleman, founder of the Coleman Lantern Company and creator of the famous Coleman gasoline lantern. At the age of eighty-four Coleman told Roberts how he went from pauper to millionaire overnight.

As a young man W. C. loved to sell. He tried everything from newspapers to typewriters. One day a man showed him a gasoline lantern and offered young Coleman the entire franchise for a thousand dollars. Liking what he saw, W. C. said, "I'll take it." He invested all he had, borrowed all he could, and started over his territory.

Then came the most shocking disappointment of W. C. Coleman's young career. Almost every storekeeper in his territory had bought a gasoline lantern already, but nobody used them. Repeatedly he heard the same story, "Don't try to sell me that thing. I have one hanging in the barn right now and it doesn't work. You can't keep it lighted."

He went to his hotel room and sat in the darkness. From his window he could see people moving around in the store across the street. The store was in the semidarkness of three kerosene lanterns. Young W. C. lit his gasoline lantern and light flooded the room. His eyes shifted from his blazing lantern to the dark store across the street.

Then the thought hit him: "I'll stop selling lamps and start selling light." He raced across the street into the store. The owner said, "I told you I don't want your lanterns." Coleman replied, "I'm not selling lamps, I'm selling light. You pay me to light your store. If the lamps don't work, that's my problem. You pay for the light."

He hung three lamps in the store, lit them, and returned to

his hotel. He put a bucket of water in the center of his room and began watching the lights across the street. A lamp would flicker and go out. He would run, replace the darkened lamp, then fill the faulty lamp with air, hold it beneath the water, find the leak, solder it, fill it with gas and take it back to the store.

A million-dollar decision to sell light instead of lamps.

Soldier; Patriotism

Dedication

It is told that in World War II there was a young American soldier who was seriously wounded. His arm was so badly shattered that it had to be amputated. He was a magnificent specimen of manhood, and the surgeon was grieved that the lad must go through life crippled. So he waited beside the injured man's bed to tell him the bad news when he regained consciousness. When the lad's eyes finally focused, the surgeon gently said to him: "I am sorry to tell you that you have lost your arm." "Sir," said the young man, "I did not lose it; I gave it . . . for the United States."

Child Abuse;
Loving Your Enemies

Depravity

Jeffery Lansdown died when he was five-years-old. He was beaten to death by his stepfather. As reported by the press, Jeffery's nude, animal-ravaged remains were found at the bottom of an embankment near a desert road. For three weeks prior to his death, the boy had suffered savage mistreatment at the hands of Ronald Fouquet, the stepfather. The mother claimed that she dared not interfere because she feared he would harm her other children.

Jeffery had been polishing one of his father's shoes, and it had fallen out of the window to the street below. The mother could not retrieve it because her husband would not permit her to leave the house when he was away. Later in the day the boy accidentally upset a can of paint.

When Fouquet discovered his shoe missing, he beat the boy mercilessly with a belt and ordered him to stand in a corner. Later, when he discovered the spilled paint, he beat him again, and refused to allow him to eat dinner.

The mother told how the father not only beat the child, jumping up and down on his stomach, but forced him to stand in the corner for days at a time with wrists taped together and hands tied to a doorknob to prevent the child from stooping or sitting. As his wife related the story to the jury, Fouquet sat smirking.

Little Jeffery died after two weeks of torture at the hands of a depraved, sadistic animal in the name of discipline. On the day he died, Fouquet ordered Jeffery to crawl back and forth between the bathroom and living room until exhausted. He gave the youngster a cold shower, jumped on his stomach, then sat down with beer in hand to watch television. Several feet away five-year-old Jeffery wept. In moments he lay dead beside a joking stepfather.

Later police asked the mother what her son had said when Fouquet had threatened to kill him. The mother sobbed, "Jeff just said, 'Daddy, I love you.'"

Depression

Senator Thomas Eagleton of Missouri was forced to with-

58

draw as the Democratic vice-presidential nominee in 1972 after party leaders learned he had undergone electroshock treatment for depression. Was he fit, we asked, to withstand the mental rigors of executive decision-making?

Yet more than a century ago, one of our most beloved presidents, Abraham Lincoln, endured fitful moods of despair in which he saw visions of his own coffin. Melancholy was the common term applied to Lincoln's moods. Today we would probably recognize them as signs of depression.

Winston Churchill acknowledged that he was periodically overtaken by the "black dog" of depression. Painter Vincent Van Gogh cut off his ear in a period of despair. Martin Luther wrote that recurrent melancholy brought him "close to the gates of death and hell . . . shaken by desperation and blasphemy of God."

How thankful we as Christians should be that in our black moods of depression we can turn to our loving Lord for solace and encouragement. He, having undergone the same temptations can sustain and strengthen us.

Parents; Wedding

Determination

Motorists and pedestrians stared in disbelief as a pickup truck passed along the street in Glendora, California. Riding in a bed in the back of the open truck was a man whose cast-encased leg was suspended in the air. Three young men accompanied the patient — one held his foot, one held the weights so they wouldn't swing, and the third kept the bed from moving.

Arthur Douglas was on his way to his son's wedding.

Douglas had been hospitalized after he broke his hip in a fall six weeks before the wedding. The doctor consented to the unusual travel arrangements, and the proud father viewed the wedding from an usher's room adjoining the nave.

"I'd rather not make the trip again," he commented after it was over. "But I would if it came to that. After all it's a once-in-a-lifetime event for a parent to see his child married. We felt it was important for me to be there."

Vacation

Dilemma

When Arthur Brisbane was about to complete fifty years of journalism, Mr. Hearst, his employer, urged him to take a six months vacation with pay in full. This magnanimous offer Brisbane refused to accept, saying there were two reasons for his decision.

"The first reason," he said, "is that if I quit writing my column for six months it might affect the circulation of your newspapers. The second reason is that it might not affect the circulation."

Devil

Discouragement

There is an old-time fable that the devil once held a sale and offered all the tools of his trade to anyone who would pay his price. They were spread out on the table, each one properly labeled — hatred, malice, envy, despair, sickness, sensuality — all weapons that everyone knows so well.

But off on the side, apart from the rest, lay a harmless-looking, wedge-shaped instrument marked "Discouragement." It was old and worn-looking, but it was priced far above the rest. When asked the reason why, the devil answered:

"Because I can use this tool so much more easily than the others. No one knows that it belongs to me, so with it I can open doors that are bolted tight against the others. Once I get inside I can use any tool that suits me best."

Robert Collier
The Secret of the Ages

Diversity

The French poet Jean Cocteau found out early in life why diversity is better than uniformity.

As a young man, M. Cocteau was designing a stage set which required a tree as background. He spent night after night in the theater basement cutting out individual leaves for his creation.

Then a wealthy friend, whose father owned a factory, approached him with another idea.

"Give me the design of the leaf," he said, "and in three days you will have thousands of them here."

After his friend's return, they pasted the multitude of identical leaves onto the branches.

The result, M. Cocteau recalled, was "the most boring package of flat, uninteresting forms one can see."

At last he understood why God has made each leaf of a tree and each man in the world different from any other.

Doctors

One late afternoon in Korea a doctor emerged from the operating room, tired, with beads of perspiration dripping from his forehead. His lips were almost purple with fatigue. He was asked by an onlooker how much he would have received for such a delicate operation in America.

"Perhaps four-hundred dollars," he replied.

Then came the question, "How much will you receive from this Korean woman?"

The doctor hesitated, then replied, "Nothing but her gratitude and the Master's smile."

Doctors

"Who is your family doctor?"

"I can't tell you."

"Why not? Don't you know his name?"

"Yes, Dr. Phillips used to be our family doctor but now mother goes to an eye specialist; father goes to a stomach specialist; my sister goes to a throat specialist; my brother is in the care of a lung specialist; and I'm taking treatments from an osteopath."

Doctors

The coroner called up the new doctor to advise him that he had made a slight mistake in filling out a death certificate. "I know these forms are complicated," he chuckled, "but you mustn't sign your name in the space marked 'Cause of Death.'"

"I may be new at this game," said the doctor, "but I'm honest."

Marijuana

Drugs

In New Jersey, bird watchers reported seeing pigeons fluttering erratically. Investigation uncovered the startling fact that they were drugged after feeding on marijuana plants hidden among the foxtails and sunflowers in the Hackensack River meadowlands. It was learned that the producers of birdseed had added marijuana to their product to make canaries sing better. Housewives discarded the birds' droppings in the garbage, which was eventually dumped in the meadowlands. Some of the marijuana seeds germinated, explaining the growth of the plant in the area.

The marijuana was so thick that a truckload could be gathered rather quickly, an armful reaped in a few minutes. The average plant produces half a pound of marijuana. It was estimated twenty thousand plants were growing in the meadows, over ten thousand pounds of the stuff — enough to provide a "joint" for each of the seventeen million high school students in the country.

Ecology

Many of the 120 animals mentioned in the Old Testament have disappeared from the Holy Land during the past 2000 years. Now, however, the Israeli government is reestablishing, at 160 game preserves throughout the country, herds of gazelles and ibexes (a form of goat). It has also acquired adaxes (members of the antelope family), a dozen Somali wild asses, and several onagers, the ass Jesus rode into Jerusalem on Palm Sunday. Explains an official of Israel's Nature Preserves Authority, "We need these preserves so children can see what nature was like in Bible times."

Endurance

Dr. Albert Schweitzer was playing host to several European visitors at the hospital at Lambarene in French Equatorial Africa.

"This heat is unbearable," one visitor moaned. "What's the temperature?"

"I don't know," said Schweitzer, "we don't have a thermometer here."

"No thermometer?"

"No," replied the doctor. "If I knew how hot it was, I don't think I would be able to endure it either."

Enfoldment

God shaped His universe by curling winds,
Flaming each star with a gentle breath.
All seasons raced as one when heavy Earth
Slid from His hands, but never from His love.

All God created links itself to Him:
A distant star communes with blade of grass,
Both wrapped in His enfoldment sans a hint
Of partiality. Then how can we
Believe ourselves forsaken and alone?

Grace Marie Scott
Wayward Pen

Eternity

Complete in Me

Child, do not grieve; He is not dead.
Behold, a mystery!
The crippled body he once knew
Is now complete in Me.
Somewhat the way a butterfly,
When time has come at last,
Finds sweet and sure release from that
Which bound and held it fast.
The one you love has been set free,

Today he walks green hills;
Where yesterday he was confined,
Today his spirit thrills
To soar unhindered far above
Earth's heartache and its strife.
He is not dead. Don't weep for him.
Behold, I give new life!
Child, do not grieve, for if you look
Your eyes of faith can see
The one you cherished so on earth
Is now complete in Me!

Mary Mason

Evidence

Four old cronies were sitting in the back of the local general
store in a small New England town playing poker when the
sheriff came crashing through the door accusing, "Gambling
again, eh? This time I'm going to take you fellows in to teach
you a lesson."

The first old fellow spoke up, "Not me, sheriff, I just dropped
in to talk." The sheriff turned to the second man who drawled,
"Wasn't playin', sheriff, just visitin'." The sheriff looked at the
third man and inquired, "What have you got to say?" The third
codger languidly replied, "Not guilty, sheriff, I just came in to
warm up at the stove." The fourth man sat quietly through the
whole scene studying the cards in his hand, when the sheriff
with a smile of victory on his face blasted, "Well, you can't deny
that you've been playing cards."

The fourth old gray-hair continued to look at the cards he
was holding, then in a mocking voice asked, "Now, sheriff, who
would I be playing with?"

Jack Herbert
in *The American Legion Magazine*

Evil

This is a simple yet inspiring story in the life of Commissioner Samuel Logan Brengle of the Salvation Army to demonstrate how evil can be turned to good.

In a street meeting one evening Commissioner Brengle was struck on the head with a brick thrown by a ruffian. It was a vicious blow, and the Salvationist was almost killed.

During the long convalescence of eighteen months Mr. Brengle began to write for the *War Cry*, the Salvation Army's publication. His simple articles were on the principles of holy living, and they made a deep impression on their readers. So great was the demand that the material be placed in more permanent form that the articles were printed in the book *Helps to Holiness*, which has been a blessing to thousands across the years.

When Commissioner Brengle was at last recovered, his wife handed him the brick which had been the instrument of so much suffering. Lettered on it were the words of Joseph: "As for you, ye thought evil against me; but God meant it unto good . . . to save much people alive" (Genesis 50:20 KJV).

Example

A certain pastor moved into a new community and was attempting to make a long-distance call. He told the operator, "This is Pastor_____ , and I would like to place a call to Mr._____ in Chicago." The operator misplaced the call and got the wrong party. The pastor asked kindly, "Well, Miss, would you try again?" Somewhat flustered, she made the same mistake again. The pastor then said to her, "We all make mistakes." He then continued in a kind, understanding voice, "Why don't you just try again and see what happens?" After she put the call through, she turned to a co-worker in the office saying, "Anyone who can be that kind and understanding after all the goofs I made deserves to be heard. I am going to hear him preach."

His faith produced a double action. It helped the girl regain her composure so she could finally place the call successfully, and it also prompted her to go to church. More people are won to God and His kingdom by deed than by doctrine; more are won by demonstration than by debate.

Foundation; Personality

Failure

The township of Upper St. Clair is on the outskirts of Pittsburgh. In 1958 this township erected an attractive red brick township building to house its fire and police departments, offices, and meeting rooms.

A few months after its completion, to the dismay of the township officials and to the disgust of the taxpayers, the new structure began to show ominous cracks in the walls. Eventually the building broke apart in many places. Entire sections settled mysteriously into the ground. The trouble lay far beneath the surface. Mining operations far under the building had caused the earth to sink, gradually and quietly, but insidiously.

This is similar to what sometimes happens to people. Unsuspected causes will undermine a personality. Often these causes are out of sight. But, gradually and quietly, these unseen factors will cause a useful and attractive personality to crumble into shambles.

Failure

F

A tall, good-looking young man springs out of a boat. Walking over to some rocks on the beach, he plants a flag and piles stones around the pole.

The young man's name is Charles Edward Stuart. The place is Glenfinnan on the coast of the wild Scottish highlands. The year is 1745. Young Prince Charles is a man with a dream. He has come to lead a rebellion to depose the king of Britain, the crusty German tyrant George II, an incompetent, high-handed foreigner detested by everyone, especially the proud Highland Scots.

It seems to be an impossible cause. This slim, debonair youth, however, quickly wins over the doubters. His intelligence, imagination, and leadership inspire the clans, and he soon has an army.

Prince Charles and his Highlanders move south to Edinburgh. The crowds idolize him. Although he suffers a bad defeat at the Battle of Culloden, the prince does not give up. He secretly takes a ship to France, planning a comeback and cherishing dreams of ruling wisely and well. Scotland still romantically remembers this inspiring leader with a dream as "Bonny Prince Charlie."

Next, picture a flabby, overweight old man. He is sitting, as is his custom, in a box at the Paris Opera. He is half-drunk. He lolls in his chair, rousing himself frequently to bawl loud and lewd comments. Usually he sags in the lap of a woman everyone knows to be his mistress. Few of the other patrons pay any attention to this disgusting figure; they are used to him. He has few friends, no supporters.

Who is this coarse-mannered old drunk? He is the same man who years earlier had been called "Bonny Prince." The dreams of his youth have long since died. He has changed from an inspired, charming young leader to a fat, aged sensualist. A failure, he had allowed the dreams of his youth to die.

Miracle;
Airplane Crash; Rescue

Faith

For fifty horror-filled hours, Marilyn Foos lay trapped in the snow-covered wreckage of a chartered plane . . . near the broken body of her dead husband. Falling snow blanketed the downed aircraft and bitter cold winds swept the mountainside where Marilyn and the only other survivor, pilot Greg Bennett, wondered if they too would die. "We had nothing to sustain us but half a pack of lifesavers and our faith in God," said Marilyn. "Both of us were too badly hurt to walk off that mountain . . . and we knew there was a good chance we'd freeze to death before we were found."

The ordeal of the forty-nine-year-old Washington housewife began when doctors discovered her husband, Paul, had cancer. Surgeons operated but complications set in, and doctors told Marilyn her husband would have to be flown immediately to Seattle for treatment.

When Marilyn saw the small plane scheduled to carry them across the mountains, she had misgivings about the journey. As the plane struggled to cross Mount McDonald, Marilyn's foreboding proved tragically accurate. Thick sheets of ice formed on the aircraft's wings, dragging it to the earth. The

70

plane slammed into a tree and crashed into the ground — and there was silence. Hidden by trees and deep snow, the plane lay crushed against the mountainside.

Marilyn's heart leaped with joy as she realized she had survived, but she was plunged into despair as her husband died before her eyes. Also dead were a nurse, along to care for Paul Foos, and one of the plane's two pilots. Marilyn brushed snow from the face of the other pilot and was elated to find him alive.

Marilyn said, "I felt deep remorse for my husband. I kept wondering: 'Why, God? Why weren't we given the chance to reach Seattle and fight for Paul's life?' But Greg kept telling me, 'You've got to think of yourself now.' And as I thought of my teen-age son and daughter, I knew I had to stay alive for their sakes."

The hours dragged by and no help came. Finally, fifty hours after the crash, Marilyn heard the whirring of a helicopter and realized rescuers had spotted the wreckage. "We really scrambled out of that plane . . . I was overjoyed!" she said.

Doctors learned that Marilyn had suffered cracked ribs and a separated shoulder. Bennett had internal injuries, fractured ribs, and a broken hip. Marilyn says the terrifying ordeal has renewed her faith in God.

"I had left on the trip praying for a miracle, for the life of my husband," she said. "But I found another miracle — the rebirth of my faith in God."

Healing

Faith

Dr. Phil Miles once was skeptical about supernatural healing — but no more. For when a bizarre disease attacked his body, gnarling and paralyzing his limbs, it was faith — not modern medicine — that cured him.

71

"It was a miracle!" declared the El Paso, Texas, physician, joy shining in his eyes. "It's given me new life. I'm walking, living, laughing proof that there's a healing force much more powerful than any man on this earth!"

For seven years Dr. Miles suffered from the strange disease, which caused his arms and legs to jerk spasmodically, twisting into rigid positions.

Dr. Miles, formerly on the staff of the prestigious Walter Reed Medical Center, called in some of the finest neurologists in America. But they couldn't even diagnose his illness.

Finally, bedridden and growing worse every hour, the heartsick young physician turned in desperation to his only remaining hope — faith. He asked a Christian neighbor to come to his bedside and help him pray for his recovery.

The doctor will never forget that incredible day. Every moment, every happening is etched into his memory. "I was sobbing uncontrollably as I uttered the words of that prayer," he recalled. "And no sooner had the final words left my lips when, to my utter astonishment, my hands, which had been clenched like claws for two days, suddenly began to open. A second later the rigid muscles in my feet began to relax. I realized I was witnessing the power of the supernatural — that Christ had accepted me and was healing me."

Within two days he was back on his feet . . . and today, more than two years later, he is still healthy and working again as a specialist in obstetrics and gynecology at William Beaumont Army Medical Center in El Paso.

Dr. Miles, thirty-six, said the unknown disease, probably a form of multiple sclerosis, struck without warning in 1965. "No one can imagine the overwhelming helplessness I endured as this terrible disease sporadically attacked my nervous system, paralyzing me. Each attack was worse than the last until on January 18, 1973, every muscle in my body gave out and I became bedridden."

It was at this low point that a neighbor suggested faith healing. The physician admits that he was a disbeliever at first. "But medicine had failed for me. So on January twenty-seven I invited my neighbor over to pray with me. I told Christ I believed in Him and invited Him to come into my life. Then came the miracle — I was healed!"

Dr. William Scraggs, chief of obstetrics and gynecology at William Beaumont Medical Center, commented: "I've known Dr. Miles since 1971, and know he's had two crippling attacks of a neurological disease since then, the worst coming in January 1973. I understand that specialists suggested the disease was a form of multiple sclerosis. Now, however, Dr. Miles is healthy and hasn't missed a day of work because of that disease since the beginning of 1973. He's one of our best men."

Faith

When Reverend Ivan Lowry learned he had Hodgkin's disease, he frankly told his Louisiana congregation the truth and offered to resign. They refused his resignation saying, "When you're not able to preach, we'll pay for the pulpit supply."

As the weeks passed slowly, Lowry's strength waned, and he preached his last formal sermon. The ten-minute message was significantly titled, "Going a Little Farther."

Gradually he grew weaker and had to be taken to the hospital for the last time. Meanwhile the members of the church built a home for the pastor's family. They had lived in rural church parsonages for over thirty years, and had never owned a home of their own. Nearing the end he asked to record a message for his fellow ministers. "Brethren," he whispered, "have more faith in God's promises. Do more than ever in winning people to Christ." His voice faded away. When the message was played back at the St. Tammany Ministerial Meeting, veteran ministers wept unashamedly.

He revived enough to give instructions for his funeral. Mrs. Lowry and the children stood by his bedside stroking his skeletonlike hands. "I'm so tired. I'm going home," he groaned.

Recalling the last moments with her loved one, Mrs. Lowry said later, "I read Dr. R. G. Lee's book, *Heaven*. Our son, Bob, and I stayed with him all night and prayed for God to take him home. The next afternoon Ivan reached out his thin arms and smiled. I knew he had seen a glimpse of the beyond."

Ivan Lowry died a few hours later. His nurses, accustomed to pain and death, said, "We've never seen a man like him."

Mrs. Lowry and her fatherless children went home to the new house the church members had built for them. She is there now anticipating the time when the family will be in their eternal home together.

Cancer; Fear

Faith

A woman of great faith visited her doctor for an examination. A few days later he told her she had cancer and her days were numbered. At first she panicked and fear took over. But in a few moments she regained her perspective and smilingly replied, "Well, your days are numbered too." She realized that the doctor had not introduced any new evidence. Ironically, the woman outlived her doctor, though he was much younger than she. But the important thing was not her extended life span, but the fact that she lived her remaining years free from fear.

Faith

A small boy was riding home from Sunday school in an open trolley, reading a leaflet titled, "Faith in God." Suddenly a gust of wind rushed through the car sweeping the paper from his hands into the street. In childlike fashion he spontaneously shouted, "Stop the car; I've lost my faith in God."

"Aren't children cute!" gushed one of the passengers. Another responded, "He has more sense than most of us adults. We don't even realize when we've lost our faith in God, let alone stop our frenzied rush that we might find Him again."

Fame

A number of years ago the great Enrico Caruso was driving through New Jersey when his car broke down. While a mechanic was repairing the damage, Caruso struck up a conversation with the owner of the garage and happened to mention, "My name is Caruso."

"Hey," said the owner, "you're not the guy who's so famous, are you?"

The tenor modestly admitted that he was well-known.

"Ma!" shouted the owner. "Guess who stopped at the station? That explorer fellow, Robinson Carusoe."

Choice; Marriage

Family

"You're out in a canoe with your mother and your wife. Neither women can swim. The canoe flips over in deep water. Which woman would you save?"

75

That question was put to a group of American students at Dartmouth College — and 85 percent said they would save their wife.

But when the question was asked a group of African Students, 75 percent declared they would save their mother.

Why the difference? In Africa, the family clan is the primary unit, so a man's mother is more important than his young — and replaceable — wife, explained Dr. James Fernandez of Dartmouth.

But in the U.S., married couples form new and independent units — so the man's allegiance is to his wife rather than his mother.

Love;
Relationships; Children

Family

When I was a boy, I used to go to summer camp where every night we formed a circle around the campfire for vesper services. We used to lock arms for our circle and stand close around the fire. When a boy got there late someone would have to unlock arms and everyone would have to move over to make room for him.

Family life is like that. Whenever a new baby is born everyone has to move over and make room for him in the circle of family love. There's plenty of room in the circle (although the children don't always know it), but finding that room involves shifting relations, not only between mother and father but between children and one or both parents, and among themselves.

John Rose, M.D.
in *McCalls*

Family

At the door of her house stood a mother, her arms full of coats, and four little children at her side.

Her husband, coming down the stairs, asked why she was standing there. Handing him the coats, she replied, "This time you put the coats on, and I'll go sit in the car and honk the horn."

Children

Family

The happiest families are those in which the children are properly spaced — about ten feet apart.

Tact

Family

A genealogist, researching a wealthy client's family tree, discovered that the client's grandfather had been given the chair for murder. Dutifully, he reported his findings. "Your grandfather," he said, "occupied a chair of applied electricity at a large public institute."

Fear

In January 1960, an astounding event occurred in a tiny peasant village of Tsirkuny in the Ukraine. A smelly, sunken-jawed wretch named Grisha Sikalenko appeared one morning

77

before his shocked neighbors. Everyone thought that Grisha had died a hero's death while fighting the Germans in World War II.

Actually, the night Grisha marched away to war, he had deserted and sneaked home. His mother made a hiding place for him under the manure pile at the back of the goat shed, and for eighteen years Grisha had existed in a living grave. Twice a day his mother sneaked food to him. In winters, he nearly froze; in summers, he nearly suffocated. Year after year, he lived out his miserable existence in the reeking pit, throwing away his life, afraid to face up to the punishment for desertion.

Finally, Grisha came out of hiding, expecting to be prosecuted and horribly punished. His fears were groundless. The statute of limitations had long since made him immune from prosecution.

Tennis

Forgiveness

The tennis courts of an Iowa high school adjoined the grounds of a church rectory. Occasionally, the exuberant youngsters whammed a tennis ball over the fence onto the trim lawns. One day a player, chasing a stray ball, came face to face with a large sign which said: No Trespassing. The sign came down overnight, however, when the tennis club erected its own sign directly opposite. Theirs read: Forgive Us Our Trespasses.

Forgiveness

The men called him "Mousey" or "the Mouse." He was short, sharp-faced, and had a streak of rodentlike meanness in him. No one ever caught him, but everyone suspected that Mousey picked up things like shaving cream belonging to the other G.I.'s. A couple of times cartons of cigarettes were missed, and all evidence pointed to the Mouse.

Mousey did nothing to endear himself to the others. He whined constantly and shirked his duties in the company. Always borrowing something, he had never been known to return anything. He even broke the unwritten law of the unit ratting to the lieutenant about a couple of his buddies.

The unit was shipped to the Pacific. It was assigned to hit one of those forgotten pinpoints on the map, a tiny protrusion of Japanese-held coral that had to be bought with lots of American blood.

The action was over by late afternoon. The medics looked for American wounded among the bodies around the smoking bunkers, and they found Mousey still conscious. All they could do for him, however, was to give him a hefty shot of morphine and move on to the next man.

A chaplain bent over Mousey and tried to comfort him. Mousey whispered something. The chaplain bent over the dying boy to catch what he was saying. The Mouse was gasping, "Can I — can I — be forgiven?"

Holy Spirit

Forgiveness

A few years after World War II, two women came from Asia to visit American Presbyterian churches and to witness to what Jesus Christ meant to them. One was Mrs. Uemura, the first woman to be permitted to leave Japan after the war. The other was Dr. Llano, a woman physician from the Philippines. They came to the States separately and met for the first time one morning at breakfast. It was a painful encounter. When Dr. Llano saw Mrs. Uemura, all she could think of were the atrocities and devastation heaped on her family, her friends, and her hospital by the Japanese invaders. Remembering the terrible suffering inflicted by the Japanese, Dr. Llano could not bring herself to say a word to Mrs. Uemura.

The following morning Dr. Llano heard a knock at her door. Opening it, she was startled to find Mrs. Uemura. With bowed head, Mrs. Uemura said, "Can you forgive me for what my people did to you and your people? Will you go to breakfast with me?"

Suddenly, they found themselves in each other's arms, crying. Then they sank to their knees side by side, hand in hand. Later after they washed their faces, they went together to breakfast.

The Holy Spirit came upon them! He empowered them to do what they could not do themselves; He brought them together as the church. He still takes hold of believers — even today.

William P. Barker
They Stood Boldly

Conversion

Forgiveness

Pacing back and forth in his prison cell, Leo D'Arcangelo was deeply disturbed — who wouldn't be, facing what was ahead of him?

As a boy of eleven, he had picked a lady's handbag on a crowded trolley car. That was the start.

Five years of stealing followed before his first arrest at sixteen in a Philadelphia department store.

Shortly after release he started mainlining heroin. Then began the seemingly endless arrests: November 1954, for use and possession of drugs, January 1955, for picking pockets. Shortly after, in Los Angeles, Leo was arrested for jumping bail.

As he paced in his cell he noticed a few lines crudely scrawled on the wall: "When you come to the end of your journey and this trouble is wracked in your mind, and there seems to be no other way out than by just mourning, turn to Jesus, for it is Him that you must find."

This started him thinking.

"This is the end of my journey. What have I got to show for it? Nothing except a lousy past and a worse future. Jesus, I need your help. I've made a mess of my life and this is the end of the journey, and all the crying isn't going to change my past. Jesus, if you can change my life, please do it. Help me to make tomorrow different."

For the first time Leo felt something besides despair.

Released from prison in September 1958, Leo earned his high school diploma and then went on to graduate from West Chester State College and the Reformed Episcopal Seminary in Philadelphia.

He is presently active in prison work and as a speaker in church and youth meetings.

Josh McDowell
Evidence That Demands a Verdict

Forgiveness

The father of a seventeen-year-old youth killed by the police at the scene of a supermarket holdup extended sympathy to the officer who fired the fatal shots.

The Reverend Ollie Wilson, his wife, and three of their children used a memorial advertisement in their local newspaper to ask for forgiveness for the dead youth.

The boy, Stanley, was shot to death by Patrolman Michael Slagle after the youth allegedly pointed a gun at the policeman. A state police investigation cleared Slagle of any blame.

"I trust in some way, somehow, you'll have God-felt mercy

and forgiveness toward my son, Stan, to forgive his deed," the Wilson's ad read. "And have sympathy for Officer Slagle for the badge of sorrow he feels and will wear silently and unseen and unspoken through all the rest of the years of his life."

The Rev. Mr. Wilson is a contractor and part-time pastor of the Green Street Wesleyan Church in Lebanon, Indiana.

Freedom; Life

Free Enterprise

Free enterprise has nothing to do with politics, or wealth, or business, or class. It is a way of living in which you and I, as individuals, are important. Many little things make up this way of life.

Free enterprise is the right to open a gas station, or a grocery store, or to buy a farm, if you want to be your own boss; or to change your job if you don't like the man for whom you work.

Free enterprise is the right to lock your door at night.

Free enterprise is the right to argue.

Free enterprise is the right to save money if you wish, or to blow it all on a good time, if that is what you want.

Free enterprise is looking at a policeman to protect you, a judge as a friend to help you.

Free enterprise is the right to speak freely about anything, any time, to anyone you wish.

Free enterprise has nothing to do with how much money you have or don't have, nor what your job is, or is not.

Free enterprise means the right to be yourself instead of some nameless number in a horde bossed by a few despots.

Free enterprise is the sum of many little things. But how we would miss it if someone stole it from us.

Freedom

It takes a great deal of freedom and love to be therapeutic with a group. Many years ago when Emil Brunner, the great Swiss theologian, was lecturing in this country, it was reported that when he preached in so-called liberal seminaries he enjoyed dropping "proof texts" from the Bible, and at more conservative or "fundamentalist" schools he smoked big black cigars. He loved people enough to want to jar them out of their stereotyped thinking. He wanted them to be aware that life in Christ was broader than the particular thing they had discovered.

Bruce Larson
Setting Men Free

Friendliness

Grandmother lived far away from her family, but she wrote often and told them how much she liked where she lived. She wrote many times about her friendly neighbors, and how kind they were to her. Every Sunday she prepared a dinner for them, she said, because it made her feel like they were her children.

A month passed and her family did not hear from grandmother. Then one morning a letter arrived saying she was moving to a new house on a new street. She explained she had to move because her old house needed repairing, and she could find no one to do it for her.

The next letter sadly reported she had thought her old friends would come to visit her, but not one had come, even once. As time went by grandmother wrote less and less.

83

Another month passed without a word from her. Worried, her family decided to visit her. As they started out the door, the mailman arrived with a special delivery letter from grandmother. "I am the happiest person alive. I have just learned why my friends never came to see me. They have all been too busy fixing up my old house, so we can all be together again for our 'delicious Sunday dinners.' "

Diplomacy

Friendliness

Helen LaMance as a young wife was quite overcome at finding herself alone, halfway around the world from home with her serviceman husband. Every afternoon she would sit in the garden watching her young daughter play. Across the street a sweet-faced young woman bustled about hanging spotless linens on shrubbery in her yard, or sat working on her knitting. She would always smile at Helen who would smile back.

One day Helen saw several pieces of the laundry lying on the muddy ground. She dashed over to the young woman's house, knocked on her door, and told her about her muddy wash.

The next afternoon Helen opened her door to a gentle knock. "Please," said her neighbor, "you trinkin coffee?" In her garden she had a table set up with coffee and apple strudel, and they enjoyed what was to be the first of many pleasant visits. With one speaking mostly German and the other mostly English, they chatted for hours.

Before Helen left Germany, her good friend reminded her of the day her wash had fallen. She smiled and said, "I put the clothes there. I wanted so much to meet you — you looked like you had a friendly heart."

Perhaps diplomats need a precise knowledge of the language

to get along with another nation, but Helen LaMance is convinced that all a woman needs is a friendly heart.

Choice

Friendliness

The milkman whose route was in an exclusive residential area asked to be transferred. He complained that the houses were too far back from the road, and he had to walk down a long path to make every delivery. On top of that, the people were very unfriendly. They wouldn't so much as wish him a good day.

Eventually he was transferred to an area which, he was told, was not so exclusive. The houses were right along the streets, and the people were the friendliest in the world.

The milkman was pleased with himself as he started off on his new route. At the first house he saw a milk bottle with a note in it. The note said:

"Dear Milkman — I have a cold today. The key is under the mat. Would you let yourself in and bring the garbage can from the backyard and leave it at the door? Then feed the cat. And please leave the front window open a little bit, and tell the butcher down the street to send up two chops. The boy can put them in the window. When you are at no. 27, tell Mrs. Brown I won't be going to Bingo tonight. P.S. I don't want any milk."

Death; Resurrection

Funeral

Most physicians would not be caught inside a funeral home.

85

Yet after thirty years of serving as a physician, I was asked to hold the funeral service for one of my former patients. When the funeral director called me at the hospital and said that the family had requested me to conduct the funeral services, I was startled, apprehensive, uncomfortable, and certainly inexperienced.

In consultation one day in the hospital, I dictated a long list of recommendations to Bill and instructed him in his home care. He had advanced pulmonary emphysema (he had been a lifelong cigarette smoker) and was a respiratory cripple. Bill was happily married, a farmer, and the father of five wonderful children. After my consultation, he left the hospital, only to return in November. Then his family doctor asked me to accompany him on a daily basis to see Bill. We were able to stem the tide, relieve his right-sided heart failure, and clear up his pneumonia. He went home with a long list of instructions, including oxygen and inhalation therapy equipment. But again he developed pneumonia, and those nicotine-scarred lungs and his tired heart just would not respond to our medical attention.

From the beginning of our relationship, Bill became interested in spiritual matters. He listened to me every Sunday morning as I spoke over the local central Iowa broadcasting station, proclaiming the gospel of a redeeming Savior. One by one he obtained copies of my three books and read them. As we came to know each other better, in a shy way he would express his interest in Christianity and his approval of the biblical opinions expressed in my writings. Bill had found or refound Christ in his terminal illness. One hour before he died, each labored breath sheer agony, he asked to have his wife and five children come to his bedside. I will never know what he said, but every one of his children wrote me individual letters thanking me for what I had done for their father.

An Assembly of God minister agreed to help me with the funeral and marked the passages in his Minister's Manual. As we approached the funeral home, he increased my tenseness by stating, "This was going to be a big one." He had noticed the cars streaming toward the funeral home. Indeed, the place was so packed that people were sitting on the stairs. The service started with a prayer by my friend, and soon it was my turn to speak about Bill. I told them of his suffering, his tortured breathing, his magnificent courage, his love for his wife and family. I told them of our friendship, the loss I felt. Then I talked to them about Bill's exciting interest in the saving Christ, our conversations, and my firm belief, as a scientist, that Bill was now breathing easily in the arms of his loving God. There was not a dry eye in the funeral home, and to my embarrassment, I too shed tears as I was speaking. The Holy Spirit was there in comforting, convicting, and converting power.

Anytime I spoke at any of the churches in that community, Bill's wife and members of the family would be there. I shall never forget my first funeral and am sure that few physicians have ever been called upon to perform such an emotion-tearing function. But that is what Christianity is all about.

Piety

Futility

A young Buddhist monk sitting outside his temple two thousand years ago looked very pious with his hands clasped. He was chanting Amita Buddha. Day after day he intoned these words, believing he was thus acquiring grace.

One day the Father Prior of the temple sat beside him, and began rubbing a piece of brick against a stone. This went on day after day and week after week until finally, the acolyte was overcome with curiosity and burst out: "Father Prior, what are you doing?"

"I'm trying to make a mirror," replied the Father.

"Why," gasped the monk, "it's impossible to make a mirror out of brick."

"Yes," was the reply, "and it's just as impossible for you to acquire grace by doing nothing except chant Amita Buddha all day long."

As told by Madame Chiang Kai-shek

Love; Kindness

Generosity

Three years ago we moved from the city to a ninety-acre farm. Our closest neighbor was Anna, a seventy-year-old widow who lived alone on her farm raising sheep, vegetables, and chickens, and selling eggs. Often I would be lonely with my seven children all in school and my college-professor husband away for long hours. But my phone would always ring at 10:00 A.M., and it would be Anna calling to brighten my day. She knew everyone in the area, and gave us excellent advice on caring for the chickens and the geese we had purchased. But the kindest thing I remember happened on my first birthday in our new home.

The phone rang at 10:00 A.M. "Happy Birthday! How's your corn?"

"Not ready to pick yet. I guess I won't have any for our guests at lunch."

At 11:30 that little old lady wobbled over the hills to our house with an armful of corn and a bouquet of gladioli. She was out of breath when she said, "Happy birthday!" and presented me with her gifts of love. It was the corn she was saving to feed her children and grandchildren the next day.

Delphine Zoski

Generosity

In the 1930s my husband was working only part-time. Rent and utility bills were a problem, but most of all we worried about feeding our six children properly.

One morning I sent my young son Danny to a wholesale bakery to buy day-old bread at half price. When he had been gone more than two hours, I became worried. Then, suddenly, Danny walked in with two bags of bread and sweet rolls. He also had seventy-five cents — the quarter I had given him for bread, plus fifty cents he had earned working for two hours in the bakery.

Danny had told the Jewish owner of the bakery that his father was trying to feed six children on a part-time salary. So that kind man had asked the boy to work for him two hours each morning. Every day after that he paid Danny twenty-five cents an hour and all the bread and rolls he could carry home.

M. J. N.

Giving

Generosity

The greatest surprise of Mary's life was receiving a dollar for her birthday. She carried the money about the house and then sat down on the stairs and stared at the bill.

"What are you going to do with your dollar?" her mother asked. "Trade it for something you've been wishing for?"

"No, take it to Sunday school," said Mary promptly.

"To show your teacher?"

"No," Mary shook her head, "I'm going to give it to God — He'll be as surprised as I am to get something besides small change."

Generosity

A high school senior in Moorland, Iowa, asked friends and relatives to give her money instead of gifts as graduation presents. She wanted to send a crippled child to summer camp. As a result she was able to present a check for $130 to a local children's organization.

"It is more blessed to give than to receive" (Acts 20:35). But paradoxically, "It is in giving that we receive."

Generosity

My mother was eager to begin sewing again for the first time since an accident that paralyzed her legs. My husband took her shopping for a new Singer control which she could operate by hand, to replace the knee lever of her thirty-year-old machine. In her wheelchair at the Singer store, mama chatted happily with the salesman who showed her the various controls, and finally she chose the one she wanted.

When my husband wheeled her up to the cashier, the salesman handed the cashier the pedal and the sales slip and walked away. The girl looked at the slip and waved away my mother's money. "That was the manager," she said, smiling at mama and handing her the new pedal and sales slip. On it was written: "Happy sewing! No charge."

Bonnie Smith Yackel

God

Ralph Barton, one of the top cartoonists of the nation, left this note pinned to his pillow before taking his own life: "I have had few difficulties, many friends, great successes; I have gone from wife to wife, and from house to house, visited great countries of the world, but I am fed up with inventing devices to fill up twenty-four hours of the day."

Pascal, French physicist and philosopher, put it this way: "There is a God-shaped vacuum in the heart of every man which cannot be filled by any created thing, but only by God the Creator, made known through Jesus Christ."

God

In an address in Dallas, Texas, the beloved Corrie Ten Boom, author of *The Hiding Place*, said that many times people would come up to her and say, "Corrie, my, what a great faith you have."

She smiled when she told how she replies back to them, "No, it's what a great God I have."

God

An artist once created a most unusual painting of Jesus on the cross. The body stood out in sharp relief against a darkened background. But as one gazed at the painting, a second figure seemed to appear from among the shadows. It was as if God could be seen behind the figure of Jesus. The nails that went through the hands of Jesus went into the hands of God. The nail that fastened the feet of Jesus held fast the feet of God. The crown of thorns was somehow on God's head too.

The artist had made clear his conception that it is through the experience of Calvary that we look into the eternal heart of God. What we see during those hours of torture is a picture of God's suffering and His outgoing love.

God

On an airliner a man was working a crossword puzzle. Suddenly he looked bewildered and inquired, "What is a word of three letters with *o* in the middle meaning man's best friend?" Looking amused, his friends chorused in unison, "Dog." The man worked at the puzzle. "I think the last letter is a *d*," he sounded out. But nobody got it. Maybe they did not want to be the first with the revolutionary thought that it could be "God."

God

Beth, three, was visiting her grandparents. She was telling her grandmother about the new church she and her parents were attending. "There was nobody there I knew," she said, "except God."

Golf

At the home talent golf tournament, the club professional caught one of the members driving about a foot in front of the teeing mark.

"Here!" he shouted indignantly. "You can't do that. You're disqualified!"

"What for?" demanded the golfer.

"Why, you're driving off in front of the mark."

The player looked at the pro with pity. "Go on back to the clubhouse," he said tersely, "I'm playing my third stroke."

Gratitude

A seventy-year-old toymaker is giving his toy shop to the children of Denmark. His House of Toys, one of the biggest in the world, was started 127 years ago by his family. It was a favorite haunt of fairy-tale writer Hans Christian Andersen, as well as hundreds of thousands of enchanted youngsters who romped through the five-story toyland.

In announcing that the toy store would be placed in trust for needy youngsters, the owner said: "We earned all our money from children, so it comes quite naturally to us to give the money back to the children, especially to those who have never had the joy that toys may give."

God blesses those who show gratitude. It is a quality all of us should cultivate and apply in our workaday world. In the home, shop, office, and in every other setting, even the slightest expression of gratefulness adds a divine touch that warms and inspires.

James Keller

Leprosy; Giving

Gratitude

Visitors at McKean Leprosy Hospital in Thailand are always surprised. Although over 95 percent of the Thai people, including entering patients, are non-Christians, McKean exists because of Jesus Christ. New patients quickly realize that the medicines and care offered them are because of Him. Incredibly grateful for the Christian community at McKean (where all the staff but two are Christians with arrested cases of leprosy), almost 80 percent of the patients eventually profess their faith in Jesus Christ and are baptized. Most astounding, although these Christian lepers subsist on a tiny income from handcrafts and a miniscule government dole, every one of them in the McKean Church is a tither! The only explanation is that one gives in proportion to one's gratitude.

Kindness

Gratitude

Once a week the road sweeper came by with his brush. He

94

was a friendly old fellow; and Miss Gidding, at the Hollies, got into the habit all that summer of taking him a glass of lemonade and a slice of cake. He thanked her shyly and that was all.

But one evening there came a knock on the door of the Hollies. The road sweeper was there, a cauliflower in one hand and a bunch of sweet peas in the other. He seemed embarrassed as he said, "I've brought you these, ma'am, for your kindness."

"Oh, you shouldn't have," exclaimed Miss Gidding. "It was nothing."

And then the road sweeper said an odd thing. "Well, no," he agreed, "maybe it wasn't much, really, ma'am. But it was more than anybody else did."

H. L. Gee
in *London Epworth Press*

Greed

When Dr. Edwin St. John Ward was in charge of the American Hospital in Beirut, a Syrian came to him with a strange complaint. The man had been attacked by bandits. To save the twenty-six gold pounds he carried, his total wealth, he swallowed them. The money had so weighted his stomach that his whole digestive system was thrown out of order. He could get no good from food even if he could afford it. When Dr. Ward expressed his skepticism of the veracity of the story, the man lay down and rattled the coins so the physician could hear them clink in his abdomen. Dr. Ward operated and removed the golden sovereigns from the man's abdomen. The recuperating man's eyes gleamed as Dr. Ward handed him the newly cleaned gold pieces.

The poor Syrian's plight, both tragic and ludicrous as it was, fairly describes the condition of many people. They have gold, or gold has them, but they are starving for the real food of life.

Greed

Dr. A. J. Gordon told of a wealthy miser who was afflicted with cataracts on both eyes. He consulted a distinguished eye surgeon and after the examination was told they could be removed to restore his sight. "But what will it cost?" was the anxious question. "One hundred dollars for each eye," was the answer. The miser thought of his money, then of his blindness, and finally said, "I will have one eye restored; that will be enough to enable me to see to count my money, and I can save the expense of having the other eye operated on."

"Oh, Lord, open Thou mine eyes, that I may behold wondrous things out of Thy law."

Growth

Four hundred years ago a gardener planted a small pine tree in one inch of soil in a shallow dish. He trimmed each root and branch as the tree grew. When he died, his son took up the task, and so on down through nineteen generations. Today that tree stands, never having outgrown the original dish, in the Kuhura Gardens in Tokyo. After four hundred years it is only twenty inches high with a twisted top some thirty-six inches across.

That little tree shouts a warning to every parent. The mind and the soul can be cut back just like the tree, always with the same result: a dwarf.

Guilt

Referred to me was a woman in her late forties. Her numerous intangible and unrelated complaints were coupled with tangibly high blood pressure. I was asked to hospitalize her to investigate her medical status in greater depth. She proved difficult to handle, and as laboratory and x-ray data accrued, little evidence of organic disease was found. She evoked prolonged discussions each day concerning medications for her nervousness and pain. One morning at two A.M. she requested that the chaplain visit her. With a spontaneous outpouring recital of personal information, she handed him a sack containing innumerable sedatives and narcotic pills she had been concealing and secretly taking. She also confessed that her attractive young daughter was the result of an adulterous relationship of which her husband knew. She went on to relate that she had recently told her daughter of her illegitimacy.

Already burdened with Parkinson's disease, her husband, who loved this daughter despite such shocking revelation, had kept the family unit together. The morning following her confession of all this sordid material, she experienced an acute psychotic break. Transferred to a locked ward, she received electroshock therapy and eventually was able to make moderate adjustments in learning to live realistically and appropriately.

Guilt! Real guilt! A tortured soul, overwhelmingly flooded with guilt. Can we categorically state that there is neurotic, pathologic guilt as separate from real, theologic, moral guilt?

Guilt

During World War II two destroyers entered the Portuguese

port on the island of the Azores. The British had invoked an old treaty with the Portuguese to allow the Allies to base planes and submarines there. My destroyer was the first to enter that harbor after the treaty was approved. Of the 300 men from my ship, 131 reported to sick bay for prophylactic measures against venereal disease after returning to the ship from their liberty ashore. Many were married, including the executive officer, who demanded private and secret attention. Our ship left anchorage the next day, and as I walked about the decks I could sense and feel the quietness of remorse and guilt.

Guilt

During Billy Graham's Indianapolis Crusade a man had come to the Inquiry Room desperately seeking peace of mind through acceptance of the liberating Savior. As his unique story unraveled, his assigned counselor realized the need for supplemental help and asked for assistance. This man, a pharmacist, co-owner of a well-known Indianapolis drugstore, was a former marine who had served during World War II in the South Pacific and was now a soul tormented with guilt. His unfolding story revealed that, with a group of fellow marines, he had joined in a pact "to kill every Jap possible." Drawing blood and tasting it had sealed their covenant. Consequently they killed the enemy, not as an act of war but as an act of wanton, unprincipled, unconscionable murder. When Japanese soldiers had offered to surrender, and would have been valuable to Military Intelligence as prisoners of war, they mowed them down with no compassion. When enemy soldiers had pled for mercy, this bloody band of self-appointed assassins were without normal concern, compassion, or conscience.

Now, fourteen years later, this ex-marine would still awaken at night bathed in perspiration, ruminating over the blood-tasting ritual and haunted by the Nipponese faces begging to surrender to live for another day. He was indeed "blood-guilty" and could not comprehend how, nor believe that God could forgive him for his past crimes. Most of all, he could not forgive himself and so was in agony of mind. His sense of guilt seemed as unbearable to him as the inhuman Roman custom by which the corpse was strapped to the prisoner's body. Wherever the convict went, he could not escape the increasing stench of his disgusting burden.

"O wretched man that I am! who shall deliver me from the body of this death?" (Romans 7:24 KJV).

Guilt

A World War II story tells of a Jewish couple living under the Nazi regime in Germany. Anticipating their arrest and incarceration in a concentration camp, they made plans for the care of their paralyzed son. An agreement was reached with a one-legged veteran who, in return for caring for the boy, was to receive the lease of their apartment. The couple's arrest followed, whereupon the veteran smuggled the boy away to a mountain cabin, where he was left with a meager supply of food and certain death.

The veteran rationalized that he had fulfilled his agreement and sold the apartment lease to acquire his ill-gotten gains. A strange experience followed. One morning he noticed a lump about the size of a pigeon's egg on his forehead. He pressed the bump which disappeared only to pop out at the back of his skull. Giving it another push, it showed up over his ear. Pressured from this spot it came out again on the top of his head. He felt this was a distinct improvement, for he could now cover it with his hat.

In this parable is depicted a typical human reaction, wherein an individual's guilt, apparently successfully concealed, "pops up" in a most unexpected way. Although it may be disguised by apt dissembling, it has a disconcerting habit of suddenly appearing. Even though it may be kept "under one's hat," there is always that anticipation of someone sidling up to whisper, "Your guilt is showing."

Healing

I observed the heart's stubborn resistance in a curious case which was subsequently reported in the Indianapolis newspapers. I was standing near the rear entrance of the Methodist Hospital talking with a resident and a medical student when we noticed an older man, carrying a suitcase, come through the door. Suddenly he collapsed to the floor. Rushing to his aid, we could find no pulse, no heart-beat, no respirations. Resuscitation was immediately started with external cardiac massage and mouth-to-mouth breathing. An anesthetist appeared on the scene and pitched in to help. Two people ran the length of the hospital for the "crash cart" with its precious cache of drugs and electrical defibrillating equipment. Nine times we shocked his heart, and nine times it resisted. Then, to combat the acidosis of lack of oxygen, we injected bicarbonate of soda directly into the chambers of the heart. The tenth shock then restored a normal beat. Our patient was transferred to the Coronary Care Unit and intensively treated with antibiotics for fractured ribs and a punctured lung sustained from the prolonged, vigorous pumping on his heart. The thoracic surgeon put a tube in his chest to inflate the lung.

This man was an overweight, cigarette smoking, anginal patient who had walked with a heavy suitcase in the cold, from the parking lot, to visit his wife who was a patient in the hospital. You may suspect he had a coronary occlusion; not so, just a sick heart crying out for blood.

This man, looking fit and healthy, returned to my office for his yearly checkup. Remember those magnificent words from Ezekiel: "A new heart also will I give you, and a new spirit will I put within you: and I will take away the stony heart out of your flesh, and I will give you an heart of flesh" (Ezekiel 36:26 KJV).

Health

The army doctor was examining a prospective serviceman. "Sit down in that chair," ordered the doctor sternly.

The reluctant prospect obeyed.

"A-1," pronounced the doctor. "Next."

"What!" complained the recruit. "You haven't even examined me yet."

"Well," said the doctor, "you heard me tell you to sit down, you saw the chair, and you had enough intelligence to carry out the order. Move on, soldier!"

H

Goals

Heart

Not long ago, a survey was taken of men who had survived heart attacks in their forties. Most reported that these coronary episodes had made them confront, as never before, the whole question of life's purpose, and how to live it. Several of the men felt that having a coronary was the best thing that had happened in their lives. They felt they had been wasting their lives up to that point, and the new chance they now had to reorder their priorities might otherwise never have come. One man reported that, as one form of therapy, his doctor had given him the assignment to write a clear statement of what he wanted to accomplish with the rest of his life. For the first time in years that man seriously took stock of where he had been going and where he should be going with his life.

Another man expressed gratitude to a nurse who had had a great deal of experience in the care of heart patients. She'd been able to make him feel that he was a very fortunate man, because relatively early in life he'd been warned against what she described as "breaking your heart chasing rainbows that can't be caught and would be worthless if they could be."

Heart

Dead on arrival. In life he had been the somewhat obese, thirty-eight-year-old father and husband of a now-grieving family. For several months he had faithfully jogged two miles at night and another in the morning. One morning he came home and told his wife he thought he'd had a heart attack while jogging the night before. After uttering these words he slumped onto the floor. Thumping his chest, his wife screamed for someone to call an ambulance, but it was too late for resuscitation.

Under questioning, his wife told the medical examiner she thought he had had high blood pressure and recalled that his father had died of a cerebral hemorrhage at the same age, thirty-eight. Autopsy did, indeed, reveal an enlarged heart due to high blood pressure, a hypoplastic right coronary artery, and focal scars in the heart muscle from poor oxygen supply. What a tragedy! Just thirty-eight years of age! I know nothing of his life style, but I do know he was overweight and did not heed blatant warnings.

"Keep thy heart with all diligence; for out of it are the issues of life" (Proverbs 4:23).

"For as he thinketh in his heart, so is he: Eat and drink, saith he to thee; but his heart is not with thee" (Proverbs 23:7).

"So teach us to number our days that we may apply our hearts unto wisdom" (Psalm 90:12).

Heart

In Sudan, near the east coast of Africa, Howard Jones conducted a service for a remote tribe in the desert country. Several hundred people gathered. He took his text from John 14:1, "Let not your heart be troubled." He noticed that the interpreter had a little trouble with the text, but blamed it on the usual difficulties of translation.

After the service the translator said to Howard, "Did you notice me stumble over the first Scripture you used?"

"Well, yes."

Then his translator said, "You see, in the Sudanese language, the heart isn't the seat of the emotions; the liver is. So when I translated your words, I had to go for this: 'Don't let your liver quiver!' "

Lee Fisher
*A Funny Thing Happened
on the Way to the Crusade*

Heart

My father died sixteen days after being hospitalized for his first heart attack. The temperature hovered between 90 and 100 degrees the entire time he was in the hospital.

At his funeral one of the first persons to arrive was a thin, middle-aged woman I had never seen. She introduced herself and explained that she was a maid at Midway Hospital. While she was mopping the floor the previous day, my father asked her if it would be possible to get a glass of freshly squeezed orange juice with lots of ice in it. She said proudly that she would get it for him herself. When she returned to the room my father said, "Now you sit down and rest for a minute while you drink the juice; it's for you."

Hearing her story was like receiving a double bouquet; it expressed so well my father's characteristic kindness, as well as her own thoughtfulness in coming to tell us the story.

Alice E. Owen

Narrow-mindedness;
Church

Heaven

When the new preacher moved into town, one of the first people he met said: "I certainly hope that you're not one of those narrow-minded ministers who think that only the members of their congregation are going to heaven."

"I'm even more narrow-minded than that," replied the preacher. "I'm pretty sure that some of the members of my congregation aren't going to make it."

Hell

When Jesus spoke about hell, the particular word He used was *Gehenna.* That is the name of a place, the valley of Hinnom, outside the city of Jerusalem. In that valley strange gods had been worshiped and human sacrifices had been offered. The

Jews felt that the valley was cursed, and as a result, Hinnom became the city dump. People threw their garbage there, and fires fed on that garbage day and night. When Jesus referred to hell as Gehenna, He used a terrifying picture.

What does Gehenna tell us about hell? It tells us that it is the place of wasted lives. "Hell is the garbage dump of the universe," C. S. Lewis described it; and the city dump of any town is filled with waste, things once useful thrown away because they are now useless. Jesus warns us that this is eternally true of some lives. Have you not met people who have gained their world but have thrown away their lives to get it? Life was spent but never invested. That's the hell of it — eternal regret that mourns a wasted life.

Gehenna tells us something else about hell. It is the place where life has no meaningful relationship to others. Gehenna was a bleak valley filled with the things that people no longer wanted. As far as the citizens of Jerusalem were concerned, the refuse had no value; no one cared about it. According to the Jews, the valley of Hinnom was one place on earth that could not be redeemed from idolatry, that God Himself could not change.

Golf

Honesty

A couple of duffers were competing on the golf course one day. Things were fairly even for the first few holes. After the fourth hole, one of the duffers turned to his friend who was marking the card. "How many did you take on that one?" he asked.

"Nine," replied his friend.

"That was my hole then," said the first one. "I took only eight."

After the next hole had been played, the first duffer asked his friend the same question.

"Oh, no," said the other bitterly, "it's my turn to ask first this time!"

Death

Honesty

A father sat grim-faced through the funeral service of his four-year-old son who had died of polio. As he listened to the opening words, "I know that my Redeemer liveth," he kept murmuring under his breath, "God, I'll get back at You for this! I'll get back at You for this!" This was the first honest conversation he'd ever had with God.

Later he commented: "That was a foolish thing to say, I suppose. How could I ever get back at God? Yet it was honest and kept the relationship with God open. That was the way I felt, and it was right to clear the atmosphere and get it off my chest. For then I gradually came to myself and saw that death does have to fit into some final framework, and only God can absorb it. I know now that my Redeemer does live. And I don't think I would know it, deep down inside, if I hadn't been mad at my Redeemer once . . . and said so."

Honesty

Mark has a grandfather who smokes cigars. The bands are redeemed for premiums by the cigar company, and grandfather was happy to save them for Mark, who sent them in for athletic equipment or gifts for other members of the family.

At Christmastime Mark mailed about fifty bands for a gift for his seven-year-old sister. By mistake he received in reply a large envelope with premiums worth thousands of cigar bands, with a boy's name and Florida address attached. Clearly they had been meant for the boy in Florida but misdirected to Mark instead of the record he had ordered for his sister.

Mark knew at once he should return the premiums, although he could have simply kept them. He wrote a letter to the company explaining the mix-up and returned the premiums. To his surprise and delight he received a handwritten letter from an executive of the company thanking Mark for his honesty, explaining that the Florida youngster would not have had a very pleasant Christmas had Mark not returned the premiums. He said that the record was on its way along with two-hundred bands for Mark himself.

With the bands, Mark was able to get a basketball. But Mark realized he received much more than his reward for being honest — the realization that someone was gracious enough to write a personal letter and thank him for doing the right thing. He knows that he received more than he ever expected from the experience.

Patricia Johnson

Honesty

My friend Grace was leaving for an extended vacation. Early in the morning she went to the bank for traveler's checks and cash. When she returned home she realized that she had not counted the bills. To her shock and amazement she had exactly $100 more than she thought. Carefully she looked at her bank slip and checked the figures. But she still had $100 too much.

Quickly she went to the telephone, dialed the bank, and asked for the teller who had helped her. When she heard his distraught voice, she knew she had called at a crucial time.

After identifying herself she said, "I have some extra money here."

"You have?" he managed to say. "How much? I'm $100 short."

Grace verified the amount. In ten minutes the teller and a bank official were ringing her doorbell. The teller was no older than her own son, who was then doing military duty overseas.

"Bless you," the boy said. There were tears of relief in his voice. "My first job," he offered, "after Vietnam. I just got back." Grace told me later how happy she was when she pressed the bills into his hand.

Juanita Zachry

Diabetes; Generosity

Honor

Elsa was young, fatherless, and her mother's only support. Her mother was very ill with diabetes. Her weight was down to eighty pounds, and physicians despaired of her recovery. Although insulin had been discovered, it was still in the experimental stage. Not only was it scarce, but its price was prohibitive. The only chance for her to live was locked in the hospital safe.

Frederick Banting, who discovered insulin, was then just an earnest research scientist at the University of Toronto. In desperation Elsa wrote to him, explaining the circumstances. He immediately sent the hospital two dozen vials of insulin with his good wishes for the mother's recovery. This gift allowed the mother to live happily and normally for another five years.

Eventually the price of insulin was reduced, and they were able to buy the insulin she needed. But one grateful daughter,

Elsa, has never forgotten the great heart of a medical genius, and how his kindness gave her mother a new lease on life. Elsa comments: "Dr. Banting later received knighthood and the Nobel Prize, and I know of no one who deserved these honors more."

Humility

Hsu Chu, who came from a wealthy Chinese family, entered the China Inland Mission to be trained as a nurse. He always dressed immaculately. One day he was asked to perform a menial service, to clean and shine some shoes. He felt insulted and refused. "No gentlemen or scholar would ever do such lowly work," he said. The superintendent of the hospital took the shoes and shined them himself. Hsu Chu looked on with mixed emotions. "Come to my office with me," said the superintendent. There he asked Hsu Chu to read the thirteenth chapter of John. Hsu Chu's eyes filled with tears as he read: "If I then, your Lord and Master, have washed your feet; ye also ought to wash one another's feet" (John 13:14 KJV).

"May Jesus forgive me," he prayed. Thereafter no one scrubbed floors, washed dishes, shined shoes, or did any lowly task more joyfully than Hsu Chu.

This is characteristic of the Christian faith. Greece said, "Be moderate; know thyself." Rome said, "Be strong; order thyself." Confucianism says, "Be superior; correct thyself." Buddhism says, "Be disillusioned; annihilate thyself." Mohammedanism says, "Be submissive; bend thyself." Modern materialism says, "Be industrious; enjoy thyself." Modern dilettantism says, "Be broad; cultivate thyself." Christianity says, "Be Christlike; give thyself."

Identity

A hit tune of the last decade was "I've Got to Be Me." There is no one else we can be! But identity is an elusive quality, an internally achieved awareness of who we are and where we are going.

Writer Joan Ulanov stresses: "Each human being is an unfinished product, in transit until he is dead (and maybe even after that), and utterly unique. We are always involved, like it or not, in the suspenseful and difficult process of becoming something neither we nor anyone else ever was before."

Seeking and holding onto one's identity is a lifetime job. It exacts an unflinching honesty with self and a courageous response to reality.

"Before I formed you in the womb I knew you, and before you were born I consecrated you" (Jeremiah 1:5 RSV).

Self-acceptance; Children

Identity

A second grader in Tennessee made a good start toward a sense of self-esteem when he submitted an essay entitled "My Face" to his teacher.

"My face has two brown eyes," the seven-year-old began. "It has a nose and two cheeks. And two ears and a mouth.

"I like my face. I'm glad my face is just like it is. It is not bad, it is not good, but just right."

Liking ourselves is essential to a healthy love of self which is the basis for loving others. Take a good look at yourself. Discover and accept what has been given you. It may not be as much as you'd like to see. But growth depends on acceptance of what you have and where you're starting from.

Ignorance

Billy Graham boarded a commercial aircraft and took a window seat. A man in a business suit took the seat beside him. When the plane took off and made the first turn, the man nervously gripped the arm rests, a look of fear on his face.

Billy decided the man must never have flown before.

"Is this your first time on an aircraft?" he asked.

"No," the man answered, "I'm a commercial pilot. I work for this airline."

"Is that so?" Billy said, "Then why on earth are you so nervous?"

"This pilot nearly lost control on that first bank. Everyone else was calm because they didn't know what was going on."

Lee Fisher

Kindness; Hitchhiker

Impact

John and Mary Edwards were driving along the New Jersey turnpike when they saw a young soldier with a thumb pointing their way. They stopped and waited for him. He threw his bag into the back seat and climbed in. He sat silently, almost sullenly.

Mary smiled at him and introduced her husband and herself. He nodded. She told him that their son was a Vietnam veteran. She told him of their worries and loneliness while he was in the combat zone and how grateful they were when he returned safely. "You look a great deal like him," she said and then added, "Your mother must be very proud of you." For a moment he seemed to lose the hard look.

111

They invited him to have lunch with them; and they enjoyed his change from an attitude of tension to one of relaxation. Then he began to smile. He told them of his homesickness and frustrations in army life. They tried to console him as they resumed their journey. When they reached his destination, Mary impulsively embraced him and John pressed a folded ten-dollar bill into his hand. John wrote his name and address on an envelope saying, "When you get out of the army, come see me and I'll give you a job." There was a film in the young man's eyes as he mumbled his thanks.

Two weeks later the Edwards received a letter. In it they found a ten-dollar bill and a message from their hitchhiker. It read: "When I first met you I was bitter and desperate. I was AWOL. I hated the world and everybody in it. I had made up my mind that I would kill the first persons who picked me up. You were the first. But you were so good and kind to me that I couldn't kill you. So when you weren't looking, I took the bayonet out of my bag and slid it under the rear seat. You'll find it there."

And they did.

Kindness; Reward

Impact

Every morning at nine o'clock, the busy widow, Anna, crossed her yard in five long strides, stopped at Mrs. Frisbe's back door and turned her key in the lock. She expected to find her half-blind, elderly friend clutching the same old wheelchair, and her orphaned, retarded grandson, Johnny, near her, sitting on the worn linoleum watching television. Today was different.

Johnny was kneeling by Grandma Frisbe's wheelchair sobbing; she was stroking his head with her withered hand; and in spite of Anna's usual greeting, they were in a world of their own, scarcely recognizing her presence as she walked toward them. In the next moment, the crying stopped long enough for the old lady to control her voice to say, "The doctor says that I have to go to the hospital this afternoon — who is going to look after Johnny?"

Anna was almost relieved. She had rehearsed this very situation in her mind several times. Perhaps it was the caring for her own brood of eight, or a natural talent for getting things done, or a combination of both, but she found herself saying, "Don't worry, I'll make all the arrangements, and Johnny will be happy at our house. And when you come back — "

Mrs. Frisbe stopped her by holding up her almost transparent, trembling hand saying, "I may not be coming back." Anna pretended not to hear.

Three weeks later Mrs. Frisbe's death brought several changes. Johnny, who had enrolled in the Educable Class, had a permanent home with Anna's family, and this experience had influenced her eighteen-year-old daughter to choose a career in special education. However, her decision posed a big problem — how could she pay for it?

The college registration deadline was only two days away. Then something wonderful happened. An envelope marked Important arrived and was hastily opened. It contained a letter from the insurance company (with two checks enclosed), explaining that Mrs. Frisbe wished one to be used for Johnny and the other for any one of Anna's children who would use it for special education for the retarded. "I wonder if Grandma Frisbe knows it's my birthday?" Anna wondered aloud.

Indispensability

Sometime when you are feeling important,
Sometime when your ego's in bloom,

Sometime when you take it for granted
   You're the best qualified in the room.
Sometime when you feel that your going
   Would leave an unfillable hole —
Just follow these simple instructions
   And see how it humbles your soul.

Take a bucket and fill it with water,
   Put your leg in it up to your knee,
Pull it out and the hole that's remaining
   Is the measure of how indispensable you'd be.

You may splash all you please when you enter,
   You can stir up the water galore;
But stop and you'll find in a minute
   That it looks quite the same as before.

The moral in this quaint example
   Is — Do the best that you can,
Be proud of yourself, but remember:
   There is no indispensable man!

Anonymous

David and Goliath

Initiative

The little fellow didn't have much, while the big fellow seemed to have everything. He was heavier, taller, and had the latest and best equipment. Moreover he was the champion.

The little fellow didn't have much, but he did have something. A stone. He picked it up, did the best he could with it, and two minutes later there was a new champ. The Biblical story of David and Goliath is the very best possible illustration of what can happen when, instead of wailing about lacks and handicaps, we take whatever is at hand and put it to work.

Alison J. Smith
Live All Your Life

Lack of Love

Injustice

Rhode Island has as a ward of the state a fifteen-year-old girl who cannot find a home. Her father is rich; her mother comes from a wealthy background; and her uncle is a Midwest cattle rancher said to be worth millions.

Records in the Rhode Island Family Court provide the account of the teen-ager whose identity is being withheld by officials. According to the records, the girl's parents will not take her, even though both are wealthy.

For the time being she is in the Rhode Island Training School for Girls, where she costs the state fifty-nine dollars a day. She was sent there last year after running away from a boarding home supported by the state.

The next stop for the girl (who has lived in Connecticut, Texas, Florida, and the Midwest with a variety of guardians, a result of divorce actions) may be a residential treatment center, officials say.

Court records tell the following story of the girl's life: She lived with her natural parents (her mother was born of wealthy parents and her father is reported a multimillionaire) for the first two years of her life. Following their divorce in 1959, she went with her mother to Texas and stayed there until 1969 when her mother's second marriage broke up.

She was then sent to live with her mother's parents in Connecticut and since then has lived in eight places for periods ranging from a week to a year.

Among those homes was one with her natural father and his second wife, who eventually brought her to a Providence hospital for reasons not listed in court records. The records say the father refused to provide psychiatric treatment recommended for the girl.

Efforts to bill members of her family for her care have been unsuccessful, officials say, adding that they are considering court action.

Trains

Instructions

While at his Adirondack camp, J. Pierpont Morgan decided to return to the city one day. He telegraphed the president of the railroad that he wanted the eight o'clock train stopped at Paul Smith's station. When he arrived, five minutes before the train, the stationmaster was industriously checking figures.

"You got your orders to flag the train this morning?" Mr. Morgan asked crisply.

"No, I didn't get no orders to flag no trains this morning." The station master went right on scribbling.

"You mean to say you're not going to flag this train?"

"Nope — not without orders."

Morgan hurried into the station and emerged carrying a red flag. A whistle was heard up the track. The millionaire flourished the flag and the train came to a stop.

"You'll hear about this," J. P. Morgan told the stationmaster as he boarded the train.

"Don't get excited," was the reply. "The eight-o'clock always stops here."

James Barnes
From Then to Now

Integrity

The little railroad town of Dilworth, Minnesota, has only one high school. It also has only one Carmella Varriano. Mrs. Variano was widowed in 1952, but she put fifteen sons and daughters through high school. Thirteen of the fifteen were valedictorians, salutatorians, or just missed by a few percentage points. Seven of the fifteen are college graduates and three are in college.

To show their respect for this fine woman, the Dilworth school board honored her in a special way. On the night her youngest son and her oldest grandson both graduated from high school, Mrs. Varriano was called to the front of the assemblage. Up marched thirteen of her fifteen children, each presenting her with a bright red, long-stemmed rose. Then the chairman of the board read a citation and presented her with a high school diploma (honorary — Mrs. Varriano never got past the eighth grade). The two children who missed the presentation were Patrick, who was at the same time receiving his Navy Wings in Corpus Christi, and Consuela, a teaching nun in Bogota, Columbia. Dilworth is sorry there aren't more Carmella Varrianos. The rest of the nation could use some too.

Involvement

It was July and hot. We had just crossed the salt flats of Utah and were going to spend the night in Reno, Nevada, before heading home. After finding a motel, we dressed and searched the telephone "yellow pages" for a restaurant. We finally found one that sounded just right. When we got there, it was even better than we had anticipated. The lights were dim, and there were potted plants, dark-paneled walls, sparkling silverware, and snowy white tablecloths. Unfortunately, we were told that we would have to wait an hour for dinner. Even though we were famished, we chose to wait rather than go back out into the heat.

We went into the lounge and found a comfortable place to relax while we waited. We had only been seated about five minutes when an elderly couple approached us. The lady said, "We have reservations for six and there are only two of us. Would you care to join us?" Puzzled, we thanked them and went with them. On the way we collected another couple.

The man and his wife, it turned out, were local residents. The other couple were Californians like us, on vacation. During dinner we chatted; one couple showed pictures of their children; the other talked about their grandchildren; and we bubbled about our recent wedding. It was almost like a family gathering. Near the end of dinner I couldn't resist asking, "How did you happen to have reservations for six?"

"Oh, we do that all the time," the lady replied. "It's easier to get reservations, and besides we always get to meet the nicest people from all over."

Since then, we have done the same thing in our hometown, and as the lady said, "We have met the nicest people from all over."

Involvement

Tommy was sailing his toy boat in the lake in the park. Suddenly, in the garden nearby, he noticed an old man carefully examining the flowers. Before long the boy and the man, whose name was Mac, had started a conversation, and in the following weeks they often met in the park. One day Mac looked downcast. It seemed that his house had been condemned, and he would have to live elsewhere. "I'm a loner," he said, "and I'll never live in one of those old folks' homes."

Tommy couldn't forget the look in Mac's eyes when he'd said that. What about the big room over the garage at home, furnished like an apartment? It used to be called the "guest house," but now was just a storeroom. The boy told his parents about his friend and his needs. Soon they met Mac, and when they learned he had been a florist, and that he would be happy to care for their large yard, they were happy to welcome him as a lodger.

Now Mac lives over the garage. He cooks his own meals, and reads a lot when he isn't working in the garden. Tommy is twelve now, but there seems to be no generation gap between them. Recently the boy announced proudly, "I want to be a florist when I grow up, like Uncle Mac."

Kindness

Involvement

It was a Sunday morning in Madrid. Gorgeous pastries, croissants, palmares, and suizos were heaped on plates along the counter of the shiny Cafeteria Manila. Instead of ordering something close enough to point to, or whose name I knew, I tried to ask for "one of those over there." Cafe personnel were mystified.

Just then a dapper young man beside me offered his help. In impeccable Spanish, he ordered the bun, then folded his newspaper and left, literally before I could say thank you. And in leaving he tossed the waiter enough coins to pay for both of our breakfasts.

I was wondering how I could repay him for his kindness when I noticed a tall, blond man down the counter trying to explain something to a waitress. He was a Dutch worker at a nearby plant and had left his wallet in the hotel. He knew little Spanish and was terribly embarrassed.

The waiters beamed delightedly as I paid the Dutchman's check, telling him how someone else had begun the chain.

Marylon Moore

Jealousy

Jealousy was unmasked by William Shakespeare as a "green-eyed monster." John Dryden called it the "jaundice of the soul." King Solomon left little to the imagination when he commented, "Love is as strong as death, jealousy as cruel as hell."

The dictionary defines jealousy as "an unpleasant fear, suspicion or resentment, arising from mistrust of another."

Apart from the harm to others caused by a jealous individual, he generates within himself a destructive bitterness that corrodes mind, heart, and soul.

If we try to fill our days with an active love for God and man, we will probably have neither the time nor the inclination to succumb to jealousy.

Judgment

"When I was young and pretty much satisfied with myself," an elderly man once told me, "I spent a college vacation looking for what I called 'local color' for use in a book I planned to write. My main character was to be drawn from an impoverished, shiftless community, and I believed I knew just where to find it.

"Sure enough, one day I came upon the place, made to order with its run-down farms, seedy men and washed-out women. To top it off, the epitome of the shiftlessness I had envisioned was waiting for me near an unpainted shack, in the shape of a scraggly bearded old man in faded overalls who was hoeing around a little patch of potatoes while sitting in a chair.

"I started back to my rooming house, itching to get at my typewriter. As I made the turn in the dirt road which ran past the cabin, I looked at the scene from another angle. And when I did, I saw something which stopped me cold in my tracks. From this side I observed, leaning against the chair, a pair of crutches, and I noticed an empty overall leg hanging limply to the ground. In that instant the lazy, shiftless character I had seen was transformed into a figure of dauntless courage.

"Since that hour I have never judged a man after only one look or one conversation with him. And I thank God that I turned for a second look."

Marjorie Spiller Neagle
in *National Enquirer*

Justice

Two lawyer friends were caught speeding and were brought

before the judge. The judge said, "Now, you two lawyers are qualified, so I am going to allow you to try each other's case."

The first acting judge said to his friend, "You are accused of doing fifty miles an hour in a fifteen-mile zone. How do you plead?" "I plead guilty." he replied. "All right," decided the acting judge, "I fine you twenty-five dollars. Case dismissed." The offender paid his fine and then became the acting judge for his friend's case. "You are charged with speeding fifty miles an hour in a fifteen-mile-per-hour zone," he admonished. "How do you plead?" "Guilty, Your Honor," answered the defendant. "That will be fifty dollars," said the acting judge, "this is the second case of this type today."

Traffic Ticket

Justice

One blizzardy day the municipal court in Wichita, Kansas, was closed because of heavy snow. The following letter arrived in the clerk's office a few days later:

"I was scheduled to be in court February 23, 1971, at 12:15 P.M., concerning a traffic ticket. Well, I was there as scheduled. To my surprise I was the only one there. No one had called to tell me that the court would be closed, so I decided to go ahead with the hearing as scheduled, which meant that I had to be the accuser (patrolman), the accused, and the judge. The citation was for going 46 mph in a 35 mph zone. I had the speed alert in my car set on 44 mph. As the accuser, I felt I was going over 35 mph, but as the accused I know I was not going 46 mph. And as the judge, being the understanding man that I am, I decided to throw it out of court this time. But it had better not happen again."

Kindness

The family had been living in New Hampshire when they learned they had to move to Connecticut. The husband had been sick a long time and treatment had drained their income away until they had to use the last of their savings to purchase an old truck to transport their goods and family. They left early in the morning hoping to reach Connecticut by nightfall, where friends could help until they were financially stable again.

Unfortunately, they soon ran into trouble when the motor began pounding and stalling. Then it began to rain, and long before reaching the state line the motor quit. They pulled off the road, crowded the children into the cab, and waited despondently for a police car.

Suddenly a heavy construction truck pulled in ahead of them. "What's the trouble folks?" a hearty voice shouted. When the husband explained their situation, the driver said, "Don't worry. I'm going your way myself, so I'll just hook you behind my truck."

He pulled them all the way, even stopping at a diner where he bought food and hot coffee. When they reached their friend's home, the trucker refused to take anything for his kindness. "Who knows," he said, "around the next corner, it may be my turn to need a helping hand."

Kindness

Many years ago a family traveled from Denmark to America. Father, mother, and four children, ranging in age from four months to twelve years, boarded a crowded immigrant train in New York for their journey to Iowa. The six weary travelers were crowded into two seats.

When the conductor came for their tickets, he noted their

discomfort and tried to tell the father something, but could not make himself understood. Finally, he picked up the baby and started to walk out of the car. Of course, the entire family followed him, protesting all the way. He paid no attention to them until he had passed through two more crowded immigrant cars into one which was almost empty. Then he stopped, gave the baby back to his mother, and motioned for the family to occupy as many seats as they wished. That family never forgot the kindness of their conductor.

Humor

Lawyer

George Ade had finished his after-dinner speech, and when he had seated himself, a well-known lawyer, who was also an amateur wit, rose, shoved his hands deep into his trousers pockets, as was his habit, and laughingly inquired of those present: "Doesn't it strike the company as a little unusual that a professional humorist should be funny?"

When the laughter had subsided, Ade drawled out, "Doesn't it strike the company as a little unusual that a lawyer should have his hands in his own pocket?"

Light

One evening on a hike along a country road, someone noticed a tiny speck of light in an adjoining meadow. It was smaller than the reflection of the tiniest star on a surface of water. The light disappeared in a moment, but others appeared intermittently.

An amateur naturalist explained that the light came from the glowworm. He picked up one for inspection. It was a very small insect, emitting a light so feeble that it would be noticed only on a dark night.

In the great meadow of life there are people of whose presence we are not conscious until in some hour of darkness we see from these insignificant lives an unexpected glow of courage, faith, neighborliness, friendliness, devotion, or love. A lowly private in a losing battle performs an heroic act which turns the tide; a young man makes a home for his orphaned brothers and sisters.

A tiny glow from one life in darkness is worth a thousand of those who can sparkle only in the sunshine of prosperity and well-being.

The American Way

Listening

John Drakeford in "The Awesome Power of the Listening Ear" tells of a personal experience:

"Returning from the rural area where I was pastoring my first church, I thrilled with excitement at the prospect of seeing my former pastor. I had so many stories to tell him. Entering his office, I then sat down as I started to recount my story.

"Bubbling over with enthusiasm, I poured out my tale. To my amazement, my friend didn't even look me in the eyes. He straightened up his desk top, pushed sundry pens and pencils into place, leaned over to pull out a drawer, and moved around its contents. Now and then he half glanced my way.

"My story slowed down. Its importance gradually diminished, and finally I limped to a conclusion, made a lame excuse, and left his office. It was one of the most disappointing encounters in my life.

"In a later frank interview the man told me he had really been interested in what I had to say but just wanted to make the best use of his time, hence his tidying up effort. He might have finished with a neat desk, but he had ruined a relationship. He had not learned to listen."

Listening

Dr. Ralph D. Nichols of the University of Minnesota has written with clarity about the importance of listening. He tells of going to a high school commencement in which, from the speaker's point of view, everything went wrong. One child began to cry, then another swelled the chorus. A small boy galloped up and down the aisle and was joined by another who chased him. Nichols had the sinking feeling that only a public speaker knows, when he realizes he has lost his audience.

The speaker tried every trick of his trade. He spoke louder, told a funny story, walked around the stage, peered intently and disapprovingly at the area of disturbance. But all was to no avail.

Then he tried his last desperate trick. He found one good listener. An elderly gentleman in the first row was looking up smiling and nodding his head. Concentrating all his attention on this one listener, the speaker gradually salvaged the situation and the speech was saved.

During the refreshment time that followed, Nichols asked the school superintendent to introduce him to the old gentleman who sat on the first row.

"Well, yes, I'll try to introduce you," said the superintendent, "but it may be difficult. You see, the old fellow is stone deaf."

Unable to hear, the deaf man had saved the day by concentrating his attention on the speaker.

Loneliness

A famous doctor was asked the most devastating disease in the world today. "Loneliness," he said. "Just plain loneliness." He went on, "The longer I practice the surer I am that there is no condition so acute, so universal. Everybody, at one time or another, is subject to its ravages. With many the disease becomes chronic. And not a few live constantly under its blight —

melancholy, bored, forlorn, friendless. Doctors can't cure it. Only the victims can."

Heart

Loneliness

Several years ago I treated an older man of Syrian background for complete heart block. Unmarried, he was getting his sexual pleasure from prostitutes. Without wife or children, he lived alone with his color television, his stereo record player, and his ill-gotten money. He was one of the top men in the numbers racket of a large midwestern city, yet what a lonely man he was. His life was held in the balance of a thin thread — a wire running from a battery planted under his skin to the right ventricle of his heart. He was alone with his money; alone with his wire, battery, and pacemaker; alone with his life-threatening heart disease; alone with his profanity about God, his occasional reference to his church . . . without God.

Ironically, he walked into my office one day, very jaundiced. His pacemaker continued driving his heart, while an unanticipated cancer robbed him of life. As he was alone in life, so he was alone in death with his battery continuing to stimulate a responding heart in the presence of a dead brain.

Loneliness

A large number of geriatric patients seem to be abandoned by their families. Creedmoor Hospital, in a borough of New York City, has unlimited daytime visiting seven days a week. Yet, on the first mild, sunny day after almost a week of steady snow and rain recently, only two of the several hundred geriatric patients in one building had visitors. A social worker says as many as half of the aged residents average only one caller a month, and some go for years without a visitor.

Not long ago, Dr. John N. McKnight, the geriatric coordinator of Creedmoor, received a telephone call from a man who wanted to know how his mother was doing. "She died three years ago," Dr. McKnight told him.

Love

We have a modern-day parable of a preacher going through a dark alley in the city at midnight. He was startled to hear a hard voice accompanied by an equally hard gun poked into his ribs: "Your money or your life."

It wasn't easy to frighten this minister for he was in the experience of perfect love. He answered gently and without excitement, "If you were in need, you could have gotten money from me at noon, without a gun. As for my life, you would not want to kill someone who loves you as much as your own mother loves you." They exchanged remarks until they reached the end of the alley, when the preacher asked, "How much do you want?" Turning away as he replied, the robber answered, "Nothing. You have given me more than money."

Love

In a book by the late Dean Brown of Yale Divinity School, the beloved disciple John is pictured in the days of his old age. Too old and weak to walk anywhere, he was carried into the church every Sabbath by his friends. At the end of every service they would help him get to his feet, and he would bless them saying: "Little children, love one another."

One day one of the church members got the idea that the old man was saying the same thing too often, like a minister repeating the same sermon over and over. But old John had an answer for that: "There is nothing more to be said. It is the final word. If we love one another, that is everything."

Love

A farmer printed on his weather vane the words *God is love.* Someone asked him if he meant to imply that the love of God was as fickle as the wind. The farmer answered: "No, I mean that whichever way the wind blows, God is love. If it blows cold from the north, or biting from the east, God is still love just as much as when the warm south or gentle west winds refresh our fields and flocks. God is always love."

Love

A small boy kept asking his father to help him build a clubhouse in the backyard. The father said he would, but each weekend he was involved in a business appointment, a golf date, some pressing homework, or a social engagement.

One day the little fellow was hit by a car and was taken to the hospital in critical condition. As his father stood at the bedside of his dying son, the last thing the little boy said with a smile was, "Well, Dad. I guess we'll never get to build our clubhouse." Of course the boy didn't want a clubhouse as much as he wanted fellowship with his father.

Bruce Larson
in *Setting Men Free*

Love

Bill Milliken lives and works on the lower East Side of New York City. God has done amazing things through his ministry in one of our nation's neediest areas. Socialists, psychologists, and theologians have often failed to achieve the kind of success

129

with people that Bill has experienced. His secret is simple. He has identified with people there! He moved from the suburbs of Pittsburgh into a tenement apartment and shared the life of his new neighbors. In the early years they stole from him (and some still do), ignored him, ridiculed him, hoping he would leave. But when they discovered that Bill had cast his lot with them, they began to trust him. He brought them the gift of fellowship, and now there is a whole company of young people and adults on the lower East Side who are living in New Testament fellowship, claiming life in Christ, and offering this life to their contemporaries.

Bruce Larson
in *Setting Men Free*

Social Reform

Love

Since 1951, a small, frail man has walked tirelessly throughout India providing the spark that has given millions of acres to that country's poor. Vinoba Bhave has done it by convincing wealthy landowners to give some of their property to impoverished farmers.

"He has proved beyond doubt," said a countryman, "that love can overcome lust for wealth and that moral suasion can be employed to persuade the rich to share their riches with the poor . . . . He is proving that the greatest social changes can be worked by love and not by violence."

Kindness

Love

A Canadian hunting guide, putting aside all thought of self, dropped everything to enable a Cleveland man to reach the bedside of his dying father one thousand miles away.

The Ohio resident was deep in the northern woods when he got word of his father's illness. He had despaired of reaching home before his father died. But the guide insisted on helping.

Leaving his job, his wife, and four-year-old daughter, the guide made the fourteen-hour drive and refused all payment for his services.

"I've never met a more wonderful man," exclaimed the grateful son. "If there were more people with his humanitarianism, we would have few of the problems we have today."

Love

A deputy sheriff told how he and three others had taken a violently insane man to a mental institution. He fought them every inch of the way. It required the full strength of all four men to control him. They dragged the struggling man down the hall and pushed him into a chair. Three deputies were holding him there when a cleaning woman hearing the noise came to observe.

As the insane man continued to struggle, the cleaning woman went over and touched him gently. He looked up at her and saw a woman of deep compassion. She put her hand on his shoulder. He relaxed and ceased to struggle. Someone brought her a chair. She sat beside him and began to talk gently, soothingly.

The deputies relaxed their grip. For half an hour the cleaning woman talked to him as one would talk to a child. His whole body relaxed. He could feel her love and concern and was responding to it. Finally he was led away by a nurse and went calmly. Love had done what the strength of four men could not accomplish.

Love

Alice Fisher was an elderly schoolteacher who lived in retirement on a small piece of property in the country. On the boundary line between Alice's lot and her neighbor's there was an old tree covered with wisteria. The neighbor asked Alice to have the tree removed but she refused.

One day when she was away, the neighbor cut down her tree, sawed it up for firewood, and put the wood in his own basement. Alice was furious and nursed her anger for five or six weeks. Then, finally, the spirit of the Sermon on the Mount entered her heart. She baked a cake and took part of it to her neighbor, only to have the door slammed in her face. Three days later she went back with some cup custards. This time the door was held ajar a few inches, but the gift refused. Alice's next offering was a bouquet of flowers from her garden, accepted with hesitant thanks.

Just a week after this last incident, the neighbor died suddenly of a heart attack, and his widow, dazed with grief, turned to Alice for help. During the next dark days the schoolteacher was able to minister to an entire family, and to be a tower of strength to them. How grateful she was that she had given in to God's urging to forget her resentment and to become a peacemaker in love.

Love

A minister called at the home of a family where the father took little interest in the church and seldom attended services. The minister hoped to persuade the man to join his wife in active membership, and carefully prepared what he had to say.

Sure enough, the following Sunday the man came to church. But imagine the minister's surprise when a few weeks later the man told him, "It wasn't your argument that moved me. But remember when we were talking little Jimmy came into the room? I was about to send him away, when you picked him up, patted him, and played a finger game with him. I thought to myself, Any man who loves little children must have something to say from the pulpit."

Love

A psychotic wife and mother picked up her husband's service revolver and shot him through the heart. He died instantly as she turned the gun on herself and pulled the trigger, penetrating her chest with a second bullet. Her eleven-year-old daughter was summoned from a nearby Christian camp, and her twenty-one-year-old daughter was precipitously hurried home from a Christian college two states away.

With no close relatives to turn to, with a critically wounded mother in the hospital intensive care unit, with a father to make funeral arrangements for, a frightened young sister to protect, and an estate to settle, this college senior was overwhelmed. But the Christian college rose to the heights of radical love and involvement. The president provided the money to send one of the professors to Indianapolis with her, where he could counsel, support, undergird, and radically love one of his students, so deeply in need. It meant loss of sleep, hours of counsel, funeral arrangements and attendance, separation from his own family, avoidance of tension with unsophisticated, uneducated relatives, the utmost in love and involvement. It meant unselfish, compassionate love.

Love

I once asked a psychiatrist friend of mine, "How can you teach people to love?" His answer was mildly surprising, to say the least. He answered the question by asking one of his own:

133

"Did you ever have a toothache? Of whom were you thinking during the distress of your toothache?" His point was clear. When we are in pain, even if it be only the passing discomfort of an aching tooth, we are thinking about ourselves.

The psychiatrist continued: "This is a pain-filled world in which we are living. And the pains that reside deep in the human hearts around us are not like toothaches. We go to bed with them at night and we wake up with them in the morning. Two-thirds of all the hospital beds in this country are now occupied by mental patients. One of every ten Americans has already been treated for mental illness. The pain inside of them simply became too deep and required professional treatment. The suicide rates in the eighteen-to-twenty-one-year age group is extremely high. Suicide ranks as the third highest killer in this age group. In the twenty-one-to-twenty-four-year age group, it is the fourth highest killer. This is a pain-filled world, and a loveless world that we live in. Most human beings are so turned-in by their own pains that they cannot get enough out of themselves to love to any great extent."

John Powell
Why Am I Afraid To Love?

Loveless

In the 1920s, a philosopher of American communism was a Jew named Mike Gold. After communism fell into general disrepute in this country, Mike Gold became a man of oblivion. In this oblivion he wrote a book, *A Jew Without Knowing It*. In describing his childhood in New York City, he tells of his mother's instructions to never wander beyond four certain streets. She could not tell him he lived in a Jewish ghetto. She could not tell him he had the "wrong" kind of blood in his veins. Children do not understand such prejudice. Prejudice is a poison that must gradually seep into a person's bloodstream.

In his narration, Mike Gold tells of the day that curiosity lured him beyond the four streets, outside his ghetto, and of how he was accosted by a group of older boys who asked him a puzzling question: "Hey, kid, are you a kike?" "I don't know." He had never heard the word before. The older boys came back with a paraphrase of their question: "Are you a Christ-killer?" Again the small boy responded, "I don't know." He had never heard that word either. The older boys asked him where he lived; and, trained like most small boys to recite their addresses in case of being lost, Mike Gold told them where he lived. "So, you are a kike. You are a Christ-killer. Well, you're in Christian territory and we are Christians. We're going to teach you to stay where you belong." They beat the little boy, bloodied his face, tore his clothes, and sent him home to the jeering litany: "We are Christians and you killed Christ! Stay where you belong! We are Christians and you killed Christ. . . ."

When he arrived home, Mike Gold was asked by his frightened mother, "What happened to you, Mike?" He could only answer, "I don't know." "Who did this to you, Mike?" Again he answered, "I don't know." The mother washed the blood from his face, put him in fresh clothes, and took him onto her lap as she sat in a rocker, and tried to soothe him.

Mike Gold recalled much later in life that he raised his small battered lips to the ear of his mother and asked: "Mamma, who is Christ?"

Mike Gold died in 1967. His last meals were taken at a Catholic Charity House in New York City, run by Dorothy Day. She once said of him: "Mike Gold eats every day at the table of Christ, but he probably will never accept Him because of the day he first heard His name." And so he died.

135

Minister

The young clergyman went into the pulpit with his head held high in the air. Somehow he got through the preliminaries, but five minutes after announcing his text he lost the thread of his discourse and was compelled to bring his sermon to an abrupt and most unsatisfactory conclusion. Consequently he came out of the pulpit humbled by his failure, and very conscious of the fact that he had made a bad impression.

"Oh, well," said a kindly deacon in the vestry afterward. "It's a pity. You see, if you'd only gone up the steps same as you came down, you'd have come down same as you went up."

Minister

A mild-mannered minister accepted the call to a church in a town where many of the church members bred horses and sometimes raced them. A few weeks after his appointment, he was asked to invite the prayers of the congregation for Lucy Gray. Willingly and gladly he did so for three weeks. On the fourth Sunday one of the deacons told him he needn't to do it any longer.

"Why?" asked the minister with an anxious look. "Has she died?"

"Oh, no," replied the deacon. "She won the steeplechase yesterday."

Minister

I know a minister whose congregation flinches against his time-worn theme: the sin of staying away from church on Sunday. One Monday not long ago this minister buttonholed one of his young parishioners with the greeting that he had missed him in church the preceding day. Then he launched into the subject of Sunday's sermon: "Son, you don't stay away from the movies because it's too much trouble to get dressed, or because you were out late the night before. Now, that's true, isn't it?"

"Yes, preacher, it is," agreed the unabashed young man. "But you don't go if you've already seen the picture."

Beth Russler

Offering; Children

Minister

Three small boys were bragging about their dads. The first boy said: "My dad writes a few short lines on paper, calls it a poem, sends away, and gets ten dollars for it."

"My dad," said the second, "makes dots on paper, calls it a song, sends it away, and gets twenty-five dollars for it."

"That's nothing," declared the third boy. "My father writes a sermon on a sheet of paper, gets up in the pulpit, and reads it, and it takes four men to bring in the money!"

Minister

It was a formal banquet and the minister had just finished

saying grace when a waiter spilled a bowl of steaming soup into his lap. The clergyman sizzled and squirmed; then remarked in anguished tones: "Will some layman kindly make some appropriate remarks?"

Miracle

One evening when Dr. Philip Blaiberg was gradually regaining his strength after his historic heart-transplant operation, Dr. Christiaan Barnard, his surgeon, entered the sterile room carrying a transparent plastic box. The box contained Philip Blaiberg's old, sick, discarded heart. The two men sat on the edge of Blaiberg's bed and examined the heart carefully. Dr. Barnard pointed out how nearly 90 percent of the organ was scarred, thickened, and useless. Then he said, "Dr. Blaiberg, do you realize that you are the first man in the history of mankind to be able to sit and look at your own dead heart?" As Blaiberg looked up, flash bulbs exploded, and the historic moment was captured for posterity.

Miracle

Bob was brought up in a middle-class home on Long Island. At twelve years of age he had secretly begun drinking hard liquor with his gang. When he was thirteen he tried marijuana, and when that novelty wore off he sniffed glue and that led to goof balls. From there he went on to heroin and LSD. He stole anything, at home or elsewhere, to support his habit. By the time he was eighteen, Bob had been on twenty-five LSD trips, his brain was damaged and he had served time in jail. Doctors, psychiatrists, and group therapy did not help him.

In desperation he went to Teen Challenge in Brooklyn where he was introduced to the power of God. That was the beginning of a miracle, for Bob found forgiveness through Christ and kicked his habit. His mind was healed and recently he expressed his desire to enter the ministry.

Miracle

The forty-five-year-old mother of three was referred to me for cardiac diagnosis. My examination of her heart indicated that she had existed all her years with a defective heart, a large opening between its upper chambers. My tentative diagnosis was verified by cardiac catheterization, and open heart surgery was recommended to correct the problem.

How well I recall the drama of the operating room scene. All was hushed as the chief surgeon and experienced controlling technician of the artificial heart equipment inventoried a complicated checklist as unoxygenated blood was tapped from the major veins entering the heart. The blood passed through the artificial heart nearby, and was returned purified to a major artery in the groin. The incision made directly into the upper heart chamber allowed us to immediately see blood bubbling through a large abnormal hole from the left to the right auricle. A stitch deftly put into each end of this defect was tightly held by the assistant to straighten the line of closure. Then, with a running suture the surgeon miraculously transformed this forty-five-year-old congenitally defective heart into a new heart.

Miser

Seeking a donation for a local charity, the two workers had

called on a well-known miser. For half an hour they pointed out the many needs of the unfortunates for whom the funds would be used. But in spite of their most persuasive pleas, the cantankerous old man sneeringly refused to have any part of it. Crippled children? What did they mean to him? Orphans? They were none of his business.

Finally the two workers left in disgust. For several minutes they were both silent. Then one burst out, "And to think that old scoundrel has money to burn."

"Yes," the other agreed darkly, "and that's just what's going to happen to it if he tries to take it with him!"

Misjudgment

One spring before the Civil War, a boy in search of work came to Worthy Taylor's prosperous Ohio farm. The farmer knew nothing about the boy except that his name was Jim, but he gave him a job. Jim spent the summer cutting stovewood, bringing in the cows, and making himself generally useful. He ate in the kitchen and slept in the hay mow.

Before the summer was over Jim had fallen in love with Taylor's daughter. When the farmer refused to let him marry her — telling him bluntly that he had no money, no name, and very poor prospects — Jim put his belongings in his old carpetbag and disappeared.

Thirty-five years passed, and Taylor one day pulled down his barn to make way for a new one. On one of the rafters above the haymow he discovered that Jim had carved his full name — James A. Garfield.

He was then president of the United States.

Missions

For nearly two thousand years the world has been made a more beautiful place to live by those who have refuted status and self to be Christ-seekers. In his book *Can I Know God?* Sangster tells of C. T. Studd, the great English cricketer, astonishing missionary. When Studd found Christ, he was planning on a law career. Within a month he gave up his plans and offered himself for immediate missionary work in China, remaining in England only long enough to address a series of meetings, and then going straight to China.

Two years after his arrival in China he celebrated his twenty-fifth birthday and inherited 29,000 pounds from his father. In a week or two he had given it all away. Like John Wesley, he feared that money might make "a home in his heart."

From that selfless missionary's efforts came the World-wide Evangelization Crusade, now supporting more than one thousand missionaries serving throughout the world. Studd said, "I will blaze the trail, though my grave may only become a stepping stone that younger men may follow."

These words sound much like Paul's: "I count all things but loss for the excellency of the knowledge of Christ Jesus my Lord: for whom I have suffered the loss of all things, and do count them but dung, that I may win Christ" (Philippians 3:8 KJV).

Mistake

After chasing the Union Army all over the map, even as far

north as Gettysburg way up in Pennsylvania, the Confederates and General Lee were terribly tired. The Southern Army, camped out at Appomattox, was preparing to wipe out the Yankees the next morning, march victoriously into Washington, and raise the Stars and Bars over the White House.

General Lee was resting at the Court House before mapping out the strategy for this final campaign. Into the Court House walked General Grant, ready to surrender. Grant was such an inconspicuous-looking man that Lee took him to be his orderly. Naturally, Lee gave Grant his sword to polish. Grant, very surprised, took Lee's sword and actually thought that Lee had surrendered. He even thanked Lee for surrendering, and General Lee, being a true Southern gentleman, couldn't go back on his word.

Wilton E. Hall

Nature

It is a sober scientific fact. The bumblebee's wing span is far too small for his abundant body, and what wings he has will not beat fast enough to lift him from the ground. Ask any aircraft designer and he will confirm that, according to all the laws of science, the bumblebee is earthbound.

But the bee has never heard of science, and his life is governed by a law far higher than the law of gravity. In defiance of logic, he spreads his stubby little wings and soars into the sunlight.

Car

Nouveau Riche

A Texas sheepherder finally struck it rich. Among other

things, he bought a Rolls Royce limousine. On his next trip to town the car salesman asked how he liked his new car. "Say, fella," said the sheepherder, "that is a real nice car. I sure do like that window that rolls up between the front and back seats." "I didn't know you had a chauffeur," returned the salesman. "I don't have no chauffeur," said the new owner of the Rolls, "but I sure do like that window. It keeps the sheep from licking my neck when I'm takin' them to market."

Obedience

A little boy was playing near a giant tree in his backyard. His father stood watching him when suddenly he saw something that galvanized him into action. "Fall on your face son, *now!*" he shouted. Without question the boy did so. "Crawl to me as fast as you can," the father ordered. His son scrambled awkwardly toward him and was soon lifted from the ground and grasped in his father's arms. Then he looked toward the tree, where he saw a giant python, its wicked head darting here and there in search of the meal that had escaped it. But for unquestioning obedience the boy would have lost his life.

Obedience

A certain woman demanded instant and unquestioning obedience from her children. One afternoon a storm came up. She sent her little son John to close the trap door leading to the flat roof of the house.

"But, mother — " began John.

"John, I told you to shut the trap."

"All right, mother, if you say so — but — "

"John!"

Whereupon John slowly climbed the stairs and shut the trap as he'd been told.

Two hours later the family gathered for dinner, all but Aunt Mary. Anxiously the mother exclaimed, "I wonder where Aunt Mary can be?"

"I know," John answered triumphantly. "She is on the roof."

Obsolescence

A middle-aged woman fell out of a window in New York City and landed in a garbage truck parked below. A Russian diplomat came along and saw her sitting there.

"American people are very wasteful," he commented. "That woman is good for at least ten more years."

Obsolescence

An American, gazing at a magnificent Spanish cathedral, asked the guide how long it had taken to build. "Five hundred years," he replied.

The American laughed. "Five hundred years? Why, in my country we could build a structure like that and have it fall to pieces, all inside of five years."

Opportunism

The Cunard Line operated the greatest fleet of passenger vessels in the world. Their names ended in the letters *ia* (Caronia, Franconia), and they wanted to name their greatest ship the Queen Victoria.

Accordingly, their representative sought an audience with

King George V. After the exchange of formalities, the spokesman for the steamship line said, "Sir, we would like your permission to name our latest vessel for England's greatest queen. We — "

But the king interrupted, smiling pleasantly. "The queen will be very pleased, gentlemen."

Hence the Queen Victoria became the Queen Mary.

Relationships

People

People. People important to you and people unimportant to you touch your life with love or carelessness and move on. There are people who leave you and you breathe a sigh of relief, wondering why you ever came in contact with them. There are people who leave you and you breathe a sigh of remorse, wondering why they had to go away and leave such a gaping hole. Children leave parents; friends leave friends. Acquaintances move on. People change homes. People grow apart. Enemies hate and move on. Friends love and move on. You think of the many who have moved into your hazy memory. You look on these present and wonder.

I believe in God's master plan for the interaction of lives. He moves people in and out of each other's lives, and each leaves his mark on the other. You find you are made up of bits and pieces of everyone who ever touched your life — you are more because of it, and you would be less if they had not touched you.

Pray God that you accept the bits and pieces in humility and wonder, and never question, never regret.

Perfection

Recently, I was talking with a patient I was seeing in consultation in the hospital. He had pneumonia, emphysema, and heart failure. After the examination I asked as a leading question, "What church do you attend?"

He answered, "None, they're all full of crooks."

I responded, "You're right, Mr. Whitt, absolutely right. That's why I'm there, because there is One who can forgive me for my crookedness." Then, I told him of a memorable experience my family and I had had as we stood before five hundred people joining their church.

The minister had said, "I have a few things to say to you who are joining our fellowship. This church has an imperfect minister. It has an imperfect board of deacons. The membership of this church is far from perfect. Nor do I wish to offend you by saying your family is imperfect. But, the one thrilling, saving, immutable fact about this church is that it has a perfect Lord." ·

Self-concept

Personality

Recently a plastic surgeon discovered that when his surgical arts had removed some physical ugliness or assisted a person to a more pleasing physical appearance the patient frequently underwent a transformation of personality. He became more confident, more outgoing, and exhibited a newly emancipated human spirit. In pursuing his investigation of this phenomenon, he turned to the inner image, as opposed to the external physical appearance, and discovered that this inner self-image controls a great deal of human conduct and happiness. In his book, *Psycho-Cybernetics*, Dr. Maltz depicts the ugly self-image as the radical cause of most human inertia, failure, and unhappiness.

Philosophy

Ann Bride, the English authoress, tells about the philosophy of an uncle which was condensed in the expression, "Let the shawl drag."

He was not an impetuous man. He liked to think things through and think of the consequences. His Boy Scout proclivities were killed off by an experience in Newport when he was a young man.

He saw a beautiful young lady walking along the beach. She wore an expensive and beautiful shawl, and he noticed that an end was dragging in the wet sand.

Taking off his hat, he bowed to her and said, "Madam, your shawl is dragging. "

She fixed a cold, unfriendly eye on him and said haughtily, "I like it to drag."

Ever after, when tempted to do an impetuous Boy Scout act, he'd slow down and say, "Let the shawl drag."

Phoniness

One of Lyndon Johnson's favorite stories concerned a Texas judge. The judge was called in the middle of the night to be told that his court had been abolished.

"By whom?" asked the judge.

"By a committee — the mayor, the head of the bar association, and the bank president," said the caller, as he named the men.

"Let me tell you about that committee," snapped the judge. "The mayor stole his way into office, the lawyer is a shyster, and the banker is a usurer like his father was before him."

"Calm down, judge," admonished the caller, "I was only kidding. No one has abolished your court."

"Now, that's not fair," said the judge, "making me say those terrible things about three of my dearest friends."

Pitfall

As the Rev. Raymond Roden describes it, "Here are the gory details of my recent descent and ascension."

Following one of last winter's blizzards, the Rev. Mr. Roden, pastor of Trinity Lutheran Church at Webster City, Iowa, was conducting graveside services in a cemetery where a propane heating device had been used to thaw the ground for the grave opening.

Apparently the heater also thawed an area around the grave because while the mourners were still being ushered into the tent canopy, a section of the ground gave way and dropped Pastor Roden into the grave under the coffin.

"Naturally I came out of that grave clawing at the sides and up over the pile of dirt which was there. In the process I was literally covered with mud. I did, however, complete the graveside services with whatever degree of decorum I was able to muster," says Pastor Roden.

Adds Pastor Roden: "Next day, as I was leading the liturgy for the second Sunday in Epiphany, I nearly broke up as the psalm for the day opened with these prophetic lines: 'I waited and waited for the Lord's help; then He listened to me and He heard me cry, and He pulled me out of that dangerous pit; out of a muddy hole.' "

Reprinted from the
Iowa Synod Lutheran

Politics

Christopher Columbus was the first politician because he didn't know where he was going, didn't know where he was when he got there, and did it all on borrowed money.

Politician

Politics

George Washington could broad-jump twenty-three feet, a record in those days. Today we have politicians who can side-step farther than that.

Politician

Politics

When a man is running for Congress, you are a friend; when he is elected, you are a constituent; when he legislates, you are a taxpayer.

Politics

A politician thinks of the next election; a statesman of the next generation. A politician looks for the success of his party; a statesman for that of his country. The statesman wishes to steer, while the politician is satisfied to drift.

James F. Clarke

Politics

When President Theodore Roosevelt was making a speech in Maine, he asked if there was a Democrat in the audience. An old whiskered man rose in the back of the room and said, "I am a Democrat." Roosevelt then asked him why he was a Democrat. He answered: "I've always been a Democrat, my father was a Democrat, and my grandfather was a Democrat." Roosevelt then said: "Then if your father had been a horse thief and your grandfather had been a horse thief, you would be a horse thief?" "Oh, no," the old man replied, "in that case I would be a Republican."

Politics

In a recent general election a heckler accused a well-known politician of being two-faced.

Without hesitation or change of expression the politician calmly replied: "I leave it to my audience. If I had two faces, would I be wearing this one?"

Poverty

Poverty is never having enough. Poverty is always running out of money, food, clothes, fuel, soap, bedding, room, time, of any way to go any place, of anything to do anything with.

Poverty is never having hope of having enough. Poverty is always knowing there is no way to get ahead, no way to save up in order to later have; always knowing that whatever little you have is wearing out, being used up; always knowing that just getting by, eating a little, keeping covered and as clean as you can, is always the best you can ever do.

Poverty is never being comfortable. Poverty is always being crowded, cold in winter, sweltering in summer, hungry, craving red meat, juicy fruit, rich milk; always living in drafts, smoke, dirt, grime, clutter; peeling paper and paint, poor places to work.

Poverty is never feeling you are part of the world, never being informed, never understanding. Poverty is always being told you are dumb, ignorant, can't understand.

Poverty is never feeling dignity or self-esteem. Poverty is always trying to be heard; being insulted, ignored, belittled, criticized, talked down to.

Poverty is never pleasant to the eyes, ears, nose, taste, touch. Poverty is always ugly: ugly houses, halls, rooms, yards, neighborhoods; bickering, yelling, weeping, cursing, jangling, garbage, rot, mold, mildew.

Poverty is never having joy or peace. Poverty is always fear: fear of the landlord, the welfare, the police, the storekeeper, the boss. It is always grief: for the man who is gone, the woman you can't be with, the children you can't do for. It is always emptiness and lack. It is always tears, yearning, sickness, depression.

Poverty is never being able to plan, never being able to see a way to do better. Poverty is always receiving too little to catch up, seeing your children sifted out and forced out. It is always hope being shattered, broken promises.

Poverty is never being considered honest or good or well-intentioned. Poverty is always being considered a crook, a deadbeat, a malingerer, a parasite. Poverty is never fully living. Poverty is always being only half alive.

This Week

Witnessing; Evangelism

Praise

Joni Eareckson is a quadraplegic who draws pictures with a pen in her teeth. For eight years she has been immobile from her shoulders down after suffering a broken neck from a dive into the shallow waters of Chesapeake Bay. Though she had become a Christian in high school through the witness of her friends in the local Young Life group, after her accident she became bitter, feeling there was no reason for living. But God saw her through those extremely difficult times and she finally decided that God must care. Through prayer and Bible study, she returned to faith in God and her life is on an upward swing.

Joni has now completed more than 250 drawings, has a line of greeting cards, and accepts orders for originals. In an appearance on T.V.'s Today Show, she shared her faith and conviction that God has a reason for her being in a wheelchair saying, "I want Him to be glorified through me." Joni uses Flair pens in her work, so the Gillette Company (owners of Papermate) has offered to underwrite much of her traveling. She writes P.T.L. under her signature on each drawing and tells those who are curious that it means "Praise the Lord." "And then I tell them why I want to praise Him. He is what life is all about."

Praise

"You're a wonderful little wife, and I don't know what I'd do without you." And as he spoke, he put his arms tenderly about her and kissed her, and she forgot all her cares in that moment. And forgetting it all, she sang as she washed the dishes, and the song was heard next door, and the woman there caught the refrain and sang also, and the two homes were happier because the man had told his wife the sweet old story . . . the story of love.

As she sang, the butcher boy, calling for an order, heard her song and went out whistling on his journey; and the world heard the whistle, and one man, hearing it, thought, *Here is a lad who loves his work . . . a lad happy and contented. I resolve to love my work!* So, because the man praised his wife, the song came from her heart, and it traveled on and on.

Praise

A few months after moving to a small town, a woman complained to a neighbor about the poor service at the local drugstore. She hoped the new acquaintance would repeat her complaint to the owner.

Next time she went to the drugstore, the pharmacist greeted her with a big smile and told her how happy he was to see her again. He said he hoped she liked their town and wanted her to let him know if there was anything he could do to help her and her husband get settled. He then filled her order promptly and efficiently.

Later the woman reported the miraculous change to her neighbor. "I suppose you told the druggist how poor I thought the service was?" she asked.

"Well, no," said the woman. "In fact, I told him you were

amazed at the way he built up this small-town drugstore, and that you thought it was one of the best-run drugstores you'd ever seen."

Prayer

Prayer is a wise and practical way to start the new year. But at the end of this year, if it turns out to be a better year than last, may we remember to praise God, who responded to our pleading. Let us not be like the man lost in the deep woods. Later in describing the experience, he told how frightened he was and how he had even knelt and prayed.

"Did God answer your prayer?" someone asked.

"Oh, no!" was the reply. "Before God had a chance, a guide came along and showed me the path."

Prayer

In a little town in the French Pyrenees is a shrine celebrated for miracles of healing. One day shortly after World War II an amputee veteran appeared there. As he hobbled up to the shrine, someone remarked: "That silly man, does he think that God will give him back his leg?"

Overhearing, the veteran turned and replied: "Of course I do not expect God to give me back my leg. I am going to pray to God to help me live without it."

Prayer

At a meeting of the Fellowship of Christian Athletes, Bobby Richardson, former New York Yankee second baseman, offered a prayer that is a classic in brevity and poignancy: "Dear God, Your will, nothing more, nothing less, nothing else. Amen."

Prayer

Shot down in the Pacific, a flier was forced to spend many uncomfortable days on a raft before being picked up. Not a particularly strong Christian until the time on the raft, he wrote back to his parents after his rescue:

"What kept me going during those days was knowing that you folks and everyone over at the church would be praying for me. I remember how you used to pray at supper for various people, dad, and I knew you'd be remembering me. I also remember how we'd always pray for the sick and the guys in the service and others on Sundays at church, but it never meant much to me. Until this past week. It's funny, but you know those prayers meant everything while I was sitting on that raft."

Prayer

A missionary, isolated and sometimes discouraged after years of thankless service in a remote jungle, wrote, "It has been an awful day, but I'm not down in the dumps. Somebody back home must have been praying for me again today."

Prayer

Christians in Africa, having no privacy in their huts to pray, would go off into the bush, each behind his hut, to speak to God. Soon, behind every Christian's hut, a little track became visible, where they walked back and forth to their places of prayer. Whenever a track became overgrown with grass from lack of use, another Christian would comment: "Friend, there is something the matter with your track."

Preaching

On Billy Graham Day in Charlotte, North Carolina, in 1968, Melvin Graham, Billy's younger brother, was given the privilege of saying a few words.

He opened with the story of the farmer who had seen the letters *P* and *C* in the sky; and being quite religious, he thought that it surely meant, "Preach Christ." So he left his farm and started preaching. After a few fruitless months, he decided he had misinterpreted the letters; they must have meant, "Plow corn." So he went back to farming.

"I don't want to make that mistake here," Melvin told the large audience. "So Billy spreads the Gospel, and I spread the fertilizer."

Lee Fisher
*A Funny Thing Happened
on the Way to the Crusade*

Prejudice

Young Dave Wilkerson tells of conducting outdoor youth crusades in South Africa.

"One of the white evangelical ministers in Johannesburg shocked me earnestly by stating 'the black man has no soul.' I cannot begin to describe the hurt I felt as I arrived in that great city and found the blacks seated outside. When I made an effort to open the stands and invite the blacks to be seated in the main sections, I was told that if I did a great many 'Christians' would walk out and I might even be asked to leave the country.

"Perhaps the most difficult moment came for me when I invited young people to the altar to surrender their lives to Christ. According to the rules, when the invitation was extended, the whites approached from one side and the blacks from the other. I whispered a prayer, 'O God, no wonder so many of these kids have given up on the church and Christianity. They have been taught they are not equal, that You have set a wall between them and it must be penetrated. Help me to break it down.'

"Those who stood before me were well-dressed, intelligent South Africans of both races. For the next two hours, I mingled with them, prayed for them, and listened as they unburdened their hearts to me. At first the black teen-agers were afraid to shake my hand. They seemed to cower at the sight of a white man walking in 'enemy territory.' But before long they put their arms around me and sobbed as they reached out to God from the depths of their hearts."

Justice; Beginning Again

Prodigal Son

Like every dedicated law officer, Deputy Sheriff Kayle Parker always tries to get his man. Recently, on one of the saddest days in his life, Parker did just that — and it broke his heart.

He arrested his own son.

"I love my son very deeply. It wasn't easy to put him behind bars," says Parker in a hushed voice. "Sometimes it gnaws at you so that you can't even sleep. But I'm a peace officer. I have had to arrest other people's kids, and I'm not about to do any different when my own son breaks the law."

Parker, fifty, arrested his son Rocky for burglary, then broke the news to his wife and other two children. "I tried to apologize," he said, "but they told me I didn't need to feel that way. His mother said she couldn't have done it, but she understood my position.

"I told her it wasn't easy. I said, 'You don't have to go up there every morning, look at your son through bars and tell him you still love him.' "

157

Earlier this year, the soft-spoken deputy of Shawnee, Oklahoma, collared his eighteen-year-old son on a tip from an informant that the boy was involved in a burglary Parker had been investigating.

On January 20, the crime was solved. Parker searched his son's room and found a stolen stereo. Rocky recalled that dramatic, heartrending confrontation: "Dad wasn't mean or anything. He just came into the living room and said, 'Son, I've got to take you in.' Pop and I had a man-to-man talk, and he looked pretty sad. He told me he loved me, to be a man and take whatever punishment I got. I'm really proud of my old man — he had to do his job. He tried to tell me what was right. If I had listened to him, I wouldn't be in this mess."

Young Parker's sentence was for three years, but two years were suspended by the judge. Soon he will be free again, and he has vowed to start life anew. Deputy Parker said, "Rocky's made up his mind he's going to make a decent life for himself. I'm proud of the way he's reacted."

Edward Sigall

Hitler; Astrology

Prophecy

Adolph Hitler was very much disturbed when a clairvoyant let it be known that she could predict the exact day of the Fuhrer's death. Since her predictions were always based on astrology and Hitler himself was a believer in the stars, he sent for the woman. After much divination the woman finally declared that the omens indicated no specific date for the death of the Nazi leader, other than it would definitely take place on a Jewish holiday.

"Which holiday?" Hitler demanded.

"I cannot be sure," the astrologist answered.

"You've got to be sure," shrieked Hitler, going into one of his well-known tantrums. "I demand that you be sure."

"What difference does it make?" shrugged the woman. "Any day on which you die will be a Jewish holiday."

Health; Illness

Proverbs

Proverbs may offer common sense or may be nothing more than distilled nonsense, but in all languages they have a way of reflecting man's beliefs. The Arab proverb, "There is no cure for death," and our own, "While there's life, there's hope," set the limits.

The Russians and the French prove their appreciation for the speed with which disease strikes and the tenacity with which it clings in the proverb: "Illness comes on horseback and leaves on foot."

To ward off dire consequences, the Chinese offer the sage advice: "If your eyes are sore and you touch them not, after ten days you will see a lot." Taking the tip, the Spanish and French follow with: "If you would heal your eye, your hands you must tie," and "You should never touch your eye but with your elbow."

Habits are targets, such as in the familiar "Early to bed, early to rise, makes a man healthy, wealthy, and wise"; the Italians' "Keep a cool head, a light stomach, warm feet, and forget about the doctor"; and the Russians' "He who eats on a full stomach digs his grave with his teeth."

Ecology isn't ignored. Look at the English, "The town for wealth, the country for health," and the Spanish, "The best water is odorless, colorless, and tasteless" and "Take running water at its source."

Long before the modern hippie, Spaniards said: "Give green fruit and unshaven men a wide berth."

All these could fall under the heading of "An ounce of prevention is worth a pound of cure." Or, as the Lebanese put it: "A drachma of prudence is worth a bushel of medicine."

But when such advice fails, the doctor comes and demands complete cooperation. After all, as the Russians warn, "If the sick man hides his ill, the physician will try in vain to cure him."

Perhaps the Chinese sum it all up with: "The doctor can cure disease, but not death; he is like a roof that can keep off the rain but not the lightning."

Christianity

Psychiatry

Christians and non-Christians have been swept up in the surge of interest in psychological help in this world of travesty, tragedy, turmoil, and trial. Year after year some new concept crowds the bookshelves and that becomes the yearly "conversation piece." We are in the *I'm O.K. . . You're O.K.* transactional analysis fad now. Yet it seems that its author and co-founder isn't O.K. Dr. Thomas Harris, author of *I'm O.K. . . You're O.K.* is in serious moral trouble. He has paid out fifty thousand dollars to a thirty-four-year-old woman, who, according to her attorney, charged that Harris kept her as a mistress at his home under the influence of drugs and drink. That was not O.K. with Patricia Ann Crocco, who says she lost her job and her husband as a result. In *I'm O.K. . . You're O.K.* Harris wrote that "resentment and bitterness" between a couple can lead to game playing. He should have included "lawsuits."

The finest system of psychology is embodied in the Christian faith, in the teachings of Jesus Christ, and from the study of the Holy Bible. We learn to forgive because we have been forgiven.

We learn to love ourselves, our neighbors, and our God. We learn to accept ourselves and others. We cease to tremble at the thought of failure, for we are the finite, redeemed children of the living Christ.

Psychiatry

The United States Army has discovered a new strategy in recent years for treating combat soldiers who have emotional or mental breakdowns. Instead of transporting them to a quiet, well-equipped army hospital far removed from the front lines, army doctors now treat them in makeshift tent hospitals only a mile or two from the battle zone. It has been found that the farther a soldier is removed from his unit the longer his treatment will take, and the less likely is his chance of recovery. The reason for this is now clear: instead of being labeled a "mental case" and becoming a statistic in an army hospital, the soldier feels that he is still a member of a fighting unit only a short distance away, and that he will soon return to it. Also, he sees himself as a sick person, not a psychotic, and this helps him to maintain his identity and self-respect.

Bruce Larson
Setting Men Free

Confession

Psychiatry

While working with Breuer, Sigmund Freud had witnessed a strange incident in his teacher's therapy. A young woman being treated under hypnosis said, "Dr. Breuer, if you would only let me talk to you and tell you how my symptoms started, I think it would help." Breuer agreed to let her talk. She expressed herself and felt relieved. They came to refer to this as the "talking cure." In the later development of this technique, his own, Freud devised his "free association" in which the patient reclined on a couch and expressed any thoughts that came into his mind in a type of freewheeling, verbalizing confession.

Free association continued to maintain the Catholic "one-to-one" relationship with the therapist, significantly seated at his "patient's" head, like the confessor out of sight. The analyst now became an authority figure of even greater power than the priest, as he searched the inner recesses of the patient's mind for the hidden repressions that caused his troubles. With an ex-cathedra authority he pontificated the reason for it all, and the patient was grateful to discover the "why" of his dilemma, even though he sometimes continued in his misery.

Military

Punishment

An army general was making an inspection of mess halls overseas. At an isolated post in Saudi Arabia, he called the mess officer, a second lieutenant, on the mat for inefficiency. After the general had chewed him out, the lieutenant turned on his heel without saluting.

"Lieutenant," the general shouted, "do you realize what I can do to you for what you have done?"

The lieutenant slowly turned around. "Sir," he replied, "I am a second lieutenant. I am in Saudi Arabia, and I am a mess officer. Just what more could you do to me?"

Punishment

"I'm going to give you the maximum punishment," the judge announced to a crestfallen defendant. "I'm not going to put you in our nice jail. Instead, I'm going to let you go free and worry about taxes, shortages, unemployment, politics, war, and the high cost of living."

Reaping

Samuel Taylor Coleridge, the great English poet, was once talking with a man who told him he didn't believe in giving children any religious instruction whatsoever. His theory was that the child's mind should not be prejudiced in any direction. Coleridge responded by taking his visitor outside to see his garden. Only weeds were growing in it. The man looked at Coleridge in surprise, and said, "Why, this is not a garden! There are nothing but weeds here!"

"Well, you see," answered Coleridge, "I did not wish to infringe upon the liberty of the garden in any way. I was just giving the garden a chance to express itself and to choose its own production."

R

Reaping

Alfred Nobel regarded his invention of dynamite as a boon to mankind. Then one morning in 1888, after the death of his

163

brother, he opened the newspaper and found, instead of his brother's obituary, his own, which the paper had printed by mistake. The obituary described him as a "merchant of death," who had amassed his fortune from the sales of explosives.

He was shocked. Was this to be the world's assessment of his achievements? Nobel decided then and there that it would not.

That same day, he revised his will, and established the coveted prizes bearing his name, awarded for the advancement of the human race.

Kindness

Reciprocity

Mary, about twenty, lived near a woman who was not well. One summer she offered to spend her two-week vacation taking her place in the home as nurse and mother. This freed Mr. and Mrs. Brown to go on a camping trip. When they returned, Mrs. Brown was rested, her health was improved, and both were very grateful.

Mary moved to another part of the city. About five years later, her employer's place of business burned down, leaving him close to financial ruin. Short-term jobs were scarce, and Mary faced at least two winter months without pay, in a cramped apartment, while the business was being relocated.

Two days after the fire, Mrs. Brown phoned Mary to tell her that her family was preparing to leave for a six-week stay in Arizona because of Mr. Brown's asthma. She asked if Mary would be interested in staying in their home, all utilities and groceries provided, to take care of their red setter. If so, they could start at once. Of course Mary went.

While they were away Mary learned from Mrs. Brown's sister that she had offered to take their dog into her home. Mary heard, too, that the Browns had not seemed to fret about getting an early start until they'd heard about the fire.

When they returned Mary asked Mrs. Brown if these rumors were true. Reluctantly, she admitted they were. "We didn't want to make our offer look like pay for what you did for us years ago," she explained, "but we are very glad we could finally make it up to you."

Recognition

Robert Henri, the well-known artist, was attending a private showing of pictures in a New York gallery. He was standing before a fine Sargent, when his attention was attracted by a brawny individual admiring the same canvas and murmuring: "They have given me a place at last."

"You in this sort of work?" Henri inquired.

"Been in it for years," answered the brawny one, "and this is the first time that I ever got on the line."

"Ah, indeed?" exclaimed Henri. "And where is your picture?"

The man pointed to the Sargent.

"That?" said Henri. "Why, Sargent painted that!"

"Painted it," sniffed the other. "Yes, I think Sargent was the man who painted the picture — but it was me that made the frame."

Maxwell Droke

Reconciliation

A minister from the North was asked to address an audience of college students, the majority of whom were black. He was warned in advance that many of them were hostile and bitter. How futile it would have been for him to offer "good advice"! And arguments would only have caused them to buttress their own positions.

The minister spoke: "I have come to ask your forgiveness. My ancestors were Englishmen, some of whom were involved in the slave trade. They sold, beat, and maimed your people. The 'animals' in the slave ships were not the Africans, stacked like cordwood in the holds, but my people with their brutish greed and cruelty.

"You cannot forgive them. Will you forgive me for them? America is my country. Its joy and accomplishments are mine. Its tragedies and blunders are mine too. High on the list of its mistakes is its treatment of the Negro . . . slavery, repression, lack of education and opportunities, white domination, ghetto conditions. These are my sins too. Will you forgive me for these, and for the public lynchings and private murders, for subtle snobbery and ostracism?"

The mood of the meeting was electric with power, and yet "broken" as falling waters. One by one members of the audience stood up to confess their bitterness, some of them even asking forgiveness of the speaker for their own hatred. New courses of reconciliation were charted that night.

Conversion; Beginning Again

Reconciliation

As a young man, Jim Vaus was expelled from a Bible institute for stealing. Next, he was "invited" to leave college when he was sentenced to jail for armed robbery. During World War II, as an army captain, he was convicted for taking Federal property. Free again and out of the army, he used his army electronics training to become a free lance wire-tapper in Los Angeles. In November 1949, he was set to give the Mickey Cohen crime syndicate a delaying electronic device that would enable gamblers in another city to place bets on winning horses before the race results were announced.

Then came his conversion in a Billy Graham Crusade. Vaus began to make restitution. He admitted stealing from firms for which he worked. To repay more than $15,000 took his car, house, almost everything he and his wife owned. Today, Vaus heads the Youth Development, Inc., which attempts to reach the gang leaders of East Harlem in New York City for Christ. Now, he is bringing the message of reconciliation to sex-stirred, drug-addicted upper East Side juveniles.

Conversion

Redemption

As a young lad, John, a hired man, came into my life. At forty-five John was an alcoholic, his path strewn with several common-law wives, venereal infections, multiple prison terms, a blight on my boyhood community. Then, one day my parents, with a band of Christians, began a prayer attack for the soul of this guilt-ridden, sin-stained lush. Without the fervor of an evangelistic meeting, without education, without the emotionalism of great music, without a pastor's pressured words, this unreconciled child of God, in the quiet of his own room, took the hand of the One who had gone to Calvary for him.

Imagine, if you can, the impact on a young boy's heart and mind of seeing the city tramp now standing in the back seat of an open car as he gave his testimony before a large crowd of townspeople congregated on Main Street. Imagine, too, the impact of watching this former derelict enter the waters of baptism in the local Baptist church, of hearing his testimony at camp meetings and in cathedrals, of seeing the hard lines of depravity disappear from his face, of noting the majestic, dynamic transformation of this man who had come to God in repentance and redemption. Gone was the alcohol, the ever-present tobacco cud in the corner of his mouth, and the common-law wives from his bed. Soon the city of Johnstown saw a transformed man become sexton of the Presbyterian church, sexton of the Episcopal church, sexton of his own Baptist church, and ultimately a respected deacon.

This was the man who had flooded the Schenectady jail by plugging the toilet then continuously flushing the water because, "I wanted to take a boat ride." What a contrast to see "Heart-changed" John now passing out tracts, faithfully visiting the Old Folks County Home every Sunday where he provided Bibles and spoke of God's redeeming love in Christ in every ward. All the psychological verbiage and intellectual theorizing of psychiatry fade into unimportance when one is privileged to witness the redemption-miracle of a formerly guilty heart.

Redemption

If there is one hymn sung more than any other while the preacher is inviting people to "come forward," it is "Just As I Am."

Probably more persons have accepted Christ to the strains of that old hymn ringing in their ears than any other gospel song. Robert Cunningham, editor of *Pentecostal Evangel*, says: "How well I recall the night I knelt and made Christ my personal Savior and my Lord. I distinctly remember repeating those words in my prayer as I asked God to cleanse me of sin and make me His forever."

Just as I am, without one plea,
But that Thy blood was shed for me,
And that Thou bidd'st me come to Thee,
O Lamb of God, I come.

Charlotte Elliott, who wrote that song, was an invalid living in England. One day Dr. Malan, a houseguest from Geneva, broached the subject of personal salvation and asked Miss Elliott whether she had ever come to the Lord Jesus Christ and accepted Him as her personal Savior. The young woman resented the question and quickly changed the subject. But it prompted her to think about the question.

Later she said to Dr. Malan, "You spoke of coming to Jesus, but how? I am not fit to come." He replied, "Come just as you are." She did so; and later, in her room, she wrote the lines of her hymn.

Sometime later she related her experience to a friend and showed him what she had written. The lines went into print, and eventually people began singing them to a tune composed by a New Englander, William Bradbury. Today the hymn is translated into many languages, and people of every color, age, and station in life have knelt before God and made it their prayer of penitence.

Just as I am, and waiting not,
To rid my soul of one dark blot,
To Thee whose blood can cleanse each spot,
O Lamb of God, I come.

Redemption

During World War II, I served on a destroyer with a crew of 300 and 18 officers. While firing on Biak in support of our troops, our sister ship, the U.S.S. *Kalk*, was bombed by four Japanese planes. A tragedy resulted with 75 casualties (24 deaths and 51 wounded — some badly burned and some mishandled). Among the dead was the ship's doctor, my friend who left his wife and five children without husband and father. We towed the battered hulk of the *Kalk* back to Hollandia where there was a destroyer tender. Three ships were tied together with mine, the U.S.S. *Stockton*, in the center.

While our ship was tied up, I visited the 36th Evacuation Hospital where I knew an anesthetist from my hometown. Also located in the 36th were a chaplain and his assistant, Lew Ayres, movie star, conscientous objector, now chaplain's assistant. I was able to arrange for services to be held aboard our ship, services attended by more than 900 men from the 3 ships. After Lew Ayres sang and gave a word of testimony, the chaplain from the Anderson Indiana Church of God said, "Men, I have only ten sermons. I'm going to ask you to vote for the one you'd prefer to hear." He gave the titles of his ten sermons, then came the vote by upraised hands. Do you know which title those men voted overwhelmingly for? After being exposed to death in all its stark, gory reality, they didn't vote for philosophy, or Christian evidences, or a "do-good" sermon; they voted for "What Must I Do to Be Saved?" During a time of life issues, the men wanted and needed to get down to basics.

Conversion

Regeneration

The professor was too polite to say that the landlord had warned him about his Protestant neighbor. The owner of the apartment had said, "He is a very zealous Protestant. He will try to convert you."

Professor Ruda's face then had creased with a soft Latin smile. "Let him. I will match wits with him. Perhaps I can convert him to be a free thinker like me. No?"

The professor felt that he had little to fear from a zealous Protestant. He knew something about religion and psychology himself. Had he not been raised in the Catholic faith, even though he no longer accepted the old dogmas? He had his doctorate in psychology and was professor of logic and researcher in psychology in the Argentine University of the South. His major field of study and teaching was in personality development. Perhaps, he thought, I will learn something by analyzing the personality of a Protestant missionary.

After attending the missionary's church and after exchanging beliefs hoping to show him his error, Ruda finally made the decision for Christ. He explains it this way:

"As a research psychologist in the field of personality development I analyzed hundreds of people. I sought to discover the inner motivation which governs the basic attitudes of living.

"But when I met Charles Campbell I knew that here was someone whose personality I could not rationally explain. Then when I became a Christian I understood the life-changing ingredient in his life was Christ. Today, the most important proof to me of Christianity is the amazing change that has come into my own life. Peace and confidence in God have taken the place of anxiety and worry. My troubles increased when I became a Christian, but Christ gave me the power to have victory over all of them."

Josh McDowell
Evidence That Demands a Verdict

Belief

Religion

At a county fair a farmer exhibited a pumpkin grown in the

exact shape of a two-gallon jug. "When it was no bigger than my thumb," he said, "I stuck it in the jug and just let it grow. When it filled the jug, it quit growing."

What the glass jug did to the pumpkin, our beliefs can do for our souls. We grow as big as the things we believe, and there we stop. Beliefs are creative, and they are restrictive. They make us what we are, and limit us to what they are.

Roy L. Smith
in *Christian Herald*

Religion

A Methodist, a Presbyterian, and a Baptist were discussing the question of the day: Which church Jesus would join if He returned to earth in our day? The Methodist was quite sure He would unite with that denomination. The Presbyterian was just as confident that He would never be anything but a Presbyterian. The Baptist concluded the discussion with, "I don't think He would change."

A local rabbi stole the punch line by commenting, "That's right; He'd still be a Jew!"

Rescue

During the 1960 Billy Graham Crusade in Sydney, Australia, a busload of people from the Outback were returning home and were at least fifty miles from any town when the bus motor broke down.

Rain was pouring down. Finally, some cheerful person said, "There's no use sitting here doing nothing. Let's take our Crusade songbooks and sing all the verses of every song until someone comes along to help us."

They were at page 49 when someone with tools came to help them. They were singing the last chorus of "Rescue the Perishing."

Lee Fisher
*A Funny Thing Happened
on the Way to the Crusade*

Resourcefulness

The church I serve has a summer ministry at a chapel on Point Judith, Rhode Island. At our first summer service the chairman of the board of deacons met me at the door with the information that there were no offering plates to be found. None of the men wore hats, and he thought it too undignified to pass a shoe. He had tried to borrow something suitable from a house nearby, but no one was at home. When I went to the chancel to begin the service, the problem was still unsolved.

Time came for the offering, and two ushers walked down the aisle wearing broad grins as they carried shiny receptacles. The resourceful deacon had borrowed two hubcaps from a parishioner's car.

Rev. W. Gordon Carter
Wakefield, R. I.

Respect

Some years ago the great football star Jim Brown tired of being a mere football star. . . . One cannot live long on the meringue of public acclaim when underneath is the garbage of insult and paternalism. But the furor that resulted grew out of his seeming appreciation of the concepts espoused by the Black Muslims. His friendship with Cassius Clay caused many to question his loyalty to cherished American ideals.

In explaining his actions and the thinking behind his involvement in an ambitious self-help project for Negroes, Brown said: "One thing you learn in football; one thing I learned: you must have respect. Liking does not matter, but you must have respect. Once you are on equal footing, then the rest can develop. Once you respect me and I respect you, then we can begin to regard each other as individuals. I don't look at you as white or black but as a man, and the individuality stands out. If liking comes after that, it is because of what you are as a person, and it all starts with respect. That is what we want to give the ghetto Negro — the opportunity to earn respect."

William E. Pannell
My Friend the Enemy

Responsibility

When George Lorrimer was editor of *The Saturday Evening Post,* there was an iron-clad rule that there must never be an off-color situation, indecent word, or unacceptable suggestion in the *Post.*

This rule was broken when the end of the first installment of Katherine Brush's "The Red Headed Woman" found the secretary-heroine having a drink with her boss at his home, his wife away, and night drawing on. To the deep shock of many readers, the second installment began with the two having breakfast together.

Editor Lorrimer prepared a form letter to answer indignant mail. It read: "The *Post* cannot be responsible for what the characters in its serials do between installments."

A.M.A. Journal

Sleep

Responsibility

A farmer interviewing a hired hand, asked his faults. "Well," the man answered, "the last fellow I worked for said I was awful hard to wake up during a bad windstorm at night."

Despite this admission the farmer hired him, but a few weeks later he had reason to remember the man's statement. A heavy windstorm hit the area, and the farmer woke instantly and went to waken the hired hand so they could check on stock and equipment. But the man would not wake up, and finally the farmer went out alone. To his amazement he found the barn doors securely fastened. The haystack was tightly anchored with a heavy tarpaulin. The lumber pile had heavy stones on top.

A great light dawned on the farmer. He now knew why his hired hand slept soundly while the wind blew hard at night.

Riches

You are richer today than you were yesterday if you have laughed often, given something, forgiven even more, made a new friend, or made stepping stones of stumbling blocks.

You are richer today than you were yesterday if you have thought more in terms of "thyself" than "myself," or if you have managed to be cheerful even if you were weary.

You are richer tonight than you were this morning if you have taken time to trace the handiwork of God in the commonplace things of life, or if you have learned to count out things that really don't count, or if you have been a little blinder to the fault of a friend or foe.

You are richer if a little child has smiled at you, a stray dog has licked your hand, or if you have looked for the best in others, and have given others the best in you.

Highways of Happiness

Generosity

Sacrifice

Ed and Ray were high school juniors. They were lively, intelligent, and friendly. Ed came from a professional home where he was given many opportunities: music lessons, books, adult conversations. Ray's father was an unskilled laborer, and his home lacked some material comforts; but there, too, reading and study were encouraged.

Both boys were scholastic leaders, and were particularly interested in creative writing. They competed fiercely for the school writer's club trophy, awarded annually for the highest number of points on papers submitted during the year. On the day of the final tally, Ed's followers joyfully announced that he had 108 points, Ray 105. Ray whispered miserably to me that he had forgotten a paper worth 10 points at home. I suggested that since the deadline was after school, he might go home at noon for his missing paper, but he only shook his head.

At four o'clock the candidates presented their portfolios and the secretary tallied points. Ed, 108; Ray 115! Ray had won. Later, I learned what had happened.

At lunchtime Ed had found out that Ray could not make the extra trip home because he had no bus pass. Ed then insisted that Ray take his bus pass and pick up the winning paper.

That was many years ago. Today Ray is happily married, the father of three grown children. Ed? He was twenty-one when he died on an icy battlefield in Korea.

Love

Sacrifice

There is an old Indian legend about a tribe from the Great Lakes region which had a long-standing tradition of sacrificing one of its maidens each year to the "great god of the waters," whom the tribe feared deeply. The practice was to draw lots among the most beautiful maidens, and the selected one was put into the river above Niagara Falls and allowed to go over the falls as a human sacrifice. One year it was the chief's daughter who drew the lot of sacrifice. The chief was a good man who loved his family. He could not violate the custom of his tribe, but what was he to do? When the fateful day came, the chief could not be found to preside over the ceremony. Some of his tribesmen began to murmur against him saying he could no longer be trusted to fulfill his responsibilities as chief. Finally, as the day's end drew near, they realized they would have to go through the ceremony without the chief, or the tradition would be broken. So they put the chief's beautiful daughter into the sacrificial canoe and pushed it into the river. To their amazement, as they did so they saw another canoe gliding into the river from the bushes where it had been concealed. In the

177

gathering twilight they recognized the person in the other canoe as their chief, the girl's father. Suddenly, both canoes were caught in the swift current at the center of the river and they went over the falls . . . together!

Sacrifice

Tigranese, king of Armenia, was taken captive by a conquering Roman army. The defeated king, along with his wife and all his children, was brought before the Roman general for the death sentence. Tigranese threw himself on his knees before the conqueror and pleaded for the lives of his family. He said to the victorious Roman: "Take me and do anything you like with me, but spare my wife and children." His appeal so moved the general that he set the entire family free.

As they journeyed away from the Roman headquarters, Tigranese turned to his wife sitting by his side, and said, "What did you think of the Roman general?"

She replied, "I never saw him."

Tigranese exclaimed, "You never saw him! You were standing in his presence. Where were your eyes?"

With tears in her eyes she answered, "They were fixed upon the one who was willing to die for me. I saw no one else."

Safety

When Dr. Menachem Monsoor of the University of Wisconsin was in Morocco on a mission to study the plight of the Moroccan Jews, he found himself confronted with the hostility of the native Arabs. His hosts were quick to reassure him that no harm would befall him by telling him that they would be with him constantly and that there was safety in numbers.

"Ah, yes," he replied. "But being a biblical scholar, I would prefer safety in Exodus."

Satan

"Satan Church" has been a reality since 1966 when Anton LaVey announced his claim to the position of "High Priest of Hell" and founded the Church of Satan in San Francisco. Today, the church boasts a membership of eight thousand plus. Mr. LaVey believes so deeply in what he is doing that he claims by 1985 all the world's religions will give way to satanism.

But, for now . . . Late one evening a shabby, bearded college youth was brought into a teen church meeting. During the prayer he became violent. Insanely he kicked the teen evangelists. When they asked, "Whom do you serve?" he cried, "God."

When asked, "Which God?" he answered, "My father."

"Who is your father?" the teens asked. From quivering lips came not the lovely name of Jesus, but the hideous name of the high priest of San Francisco's Satan Church. The troubled lad was on a demon trip.

Paul warned: "The Spirit says clearly that some men will abandon the faith in later times; they will obey lying spirits and follow the teachings of demons. These teachings come from the deceit of men who are liars, and whose consciences are dead, as if burnt with a hot iron" (1 Timothy 4:1,2 TEV).

Satan

The butler complained to his proud boss that he was greatly tempted by the devil. His boss said: "You must be a very wicked man. The devil doesn't bother me."

The butler responded: "When you go hunting, sir, and shoot into a flock of ducks, which one do you chase — the one you killed, or the one you crippled?"

"I chase the crippled one, of course. I don't have to chase the dead one."

Then the butler smiled and said, "Sir, the devil knows you are a dead duck."

The proud man's weakness was exposed quite fully.

Satan

"I am a cannibal," the long-haired youth casually told arresting officers. Stanley Baker and his twenty-year-old friend related this bizarre story to police south of San Francisco. The car driven by the young men belonged to a missing Montana social worker whose armless, legless, headless, and heartless body was found four miles from Gardiner, Montana.

When highway patrolmen picked up the two students, both were carrying finger bones. It was reported that one of the youths actually consumed the social worker's heart for lunch. After questioning, authorities discovered both belonged to a growing satanic cult.

Satan's reality in this sinful century cannot be denied. The apostle John spoke of this era in Revelation 12:12: "For the Devil has come down to you, and he is filled with rage, because he knows that he has only a little time left" (TEV).

Searching

Gliding sluggishly across the bosom of India like a great brown python is the Ganges River. Muddy and filthy, it is filled with the garbage and refuse of a hundred million people. But annually, thousands of devout pilgrims crawl on their bellies for miles doing penance until they reach its slimy banks. Then they wade into it to their waists, lift their arms heavenward, and cry aloud. What are they doing? They are seeking to make atonement for their sins. They are trying to find God. As they know it, life is one day after another of hunger and meaninglessness within the structure of their primitive society. They are trying desperately to discover sense and meaning in it all. Through this ritual they are hoping to become new persons.

Self-confidence

A Yale graduate perusing the want ads in a metropolitan newspaper found one that appeared promising. It read: "Wanted, a bright Harvard graduate, or equivalent." The Yale man wrote to the box indicated, inquiring, "When you say you want a Harvard man or equivalent, do you mean two Princeton men, or a Yale man working half time?"

Self-confidence

Famous physician and author A. J. Cronin recalls a time he was given a second chance. As a young medical student he had a professor of surgery who was harshly outspoken and critical. One day this man stopped Cronin in the hall and told him that his surgical performance was hopeless; that he might become an adequate general practitioner but never a surgeon. Cronin believed him. On completion of his medical schooling the young doctor went to a remote village in the Scottish highlands to practice. He was the only physician for miles around.

One winter day with roads blocked by ice and snow, a tree fell on the son of the local pastor, crushing his spine and paralyzing him. Cronin knew a delicate neurological operation was imperative. Without it the paralysis would be permanent. But he remembered the professor's words and was afraid to take the risk, because the slightest mistake could mean death for the boy.

The pastor himself urged Cronin to operate. He said, "I will pray for you. God will help you." Cronin refused. "All I could think of was the face of that man telling me I could never be a surgeon. But then something happened. For the first time I questioned the validity of that man's verdict. Who was he to tell me what I could or couldn't do? Doubts and fears swept away. I knew I could operate successfully. And with God's help I did."

The gospel of beginning again. That is the very heart and marrow of Christianity.

181

Self-deception

Cathy, the daughter of a well-known Washington couple, became intrigued with the hippie way of life. She started to hang around Deer Park Circle in Washington and soon began "dropping acid" with new-found friends. Her restlessness made her believe that she was being trapped by society, and she resented her mother telling her what to do. It was eight o'clock one Saturday night when her new boyfriend, Francis, told her, "I'm going to San Francisco because I'm sick of all this. I want to go and find out what's happening."

The idea excited her. She, too, was disillusioned, and anyway everyone was saying, "Go out there, it's really groovy. You always have a place to stay. Everyone takes care of you. It's warm out there."

They hitchhiked, something she'd never done before. In six days they arrived with no place to stay. Francis disappeared. Some hippies promised to take her in for a week, but they stole two hundred dollars from her. She ran away from them and met a group of kids who said they needed a couple more people to start a commune.

She described their life together: "It was really terrible. Everyone was at each other's throats. One boy was dealing heavily in speed and heroin. There were all types of kids in and around this house. We started to get uptight and a couple of kids left. They couldn't stand it anymore. We were using 'grass' and expected the house to be 'busted.' We really didn't love each other — we just tolerated each other. The whole business was like standing in front of a fog bank. There is only fog there and you can't see reality. Everyone talks about being 'hip' and they hallucinate, but all they see are mirages. Life itself became a mirage."

Sensuality

Hugh Hefner, the ingenious juggler of American symbols, is noted for his advocacy of unlimited sexual license. However, in a recent interview, Hefner admitted his distaste for a woman who actually put his philosophy into effect. Furthermore, when asked whether he would encourage his daughter to be promiscuous, he admitted his intellectual schizophrenia: "Intellectually I may think in a certain way; practically I may act in another way. I am and I remain a combination of incoherences that I uselessly try to reject." Hefner does not admit the logic of his position because he is unwilling to face a world with the philosophy he espouses! At least in his lover and his daughter he retains a sector of sanity and morality. But it is not to his credit. It only proves the basic dishonesty of the non-Christian position.

Clark H. Pinnock
Set Forth Your Case

Serendipity

Sir Alexander Fleming made his discovery of penicillin while working in a dusty old laboratory. A mold spore landed on a culture plate he was about to examine.

Some years later, he was taken on a tour of an up-to-date research lab, a gleaming, air-conditioned, dust-free, super-sterile setting. "What a pity you did not have a place like this to work in," his guide said. "What you could have discovered in such surroundings!"

"Not penicillin," Fleming observed dryly.

E. E. Edgar

Service

One day in 1954, the waitress at a Mississippi highway cafe changed the whole course of Rev. Henry Bucklew's life. As she served Brother Buck, she asked, "Aren't you the preacher who's interested in kids?" He admitted he was. "Well, I'm willing to give you my two boys. My husband and I are separated. He doesn't want them, and I can't afford them."

Utterly stunned by her words, Brother Buck managed to answer, "Keep them awhile longer. I'll see what I can do."

That night Henry and Fern Bucklew made a decision that has brought both home and happiness to scores of unwanted boys. They donated land, bought three years previously to build their own home, to the then nonexistent but soon-to-materialize boys' home, Magnolia Boys' Town.

Bucklew and his newly appointed trustees began soliciting money, labor, and materials. The community responded because it loved and trusted Henry Bucklew, the son of a tenant farmer who had worked his way through junior college before going overseas to war. In a hospital in England Bucklew felt the Lord calling him to preach, and accepted. When he returned, Henry took additional schooling, then founded the *Southern Baptist News*, the paper he still edits and publishes.

Two years later Brother Buck was framing the first building when a tousled boy addressed him. "You Brother Buck?"

"That's right."

"Heard you're building a home for boys who ain't wanted at home."

The boy, Curly, told of walking twenty miles after reading about the Boys' Town in the county paper. "My stepfather told me if I came back he'd kill me," he blurted between trembling lips.

Curly stayed and, when the home was opened, was elected

184

the first mayor and later named "outstanding boy." In April 1957, Magnolia Boys' Town was officially opened. Inside a few weeks it housed more than twenty boys, including the sons of the highway waitress. At last count there were forty-one boys.

Magnolia Boys' Town has had few discipline problems. The boys elect their own officers — mayor, councilmen, sheriff — and even make their own rules. The boys eagerly take turns saying grace at mealtime and reading the Bible at family altar each evening. On Sunday mornings they are transported to the church of their faith. "Many of the boys find Christ as their Savior after they come here," Brother Buck says.

Today, the land Brother Buck bought for his retreat is neither silent nor serene. It is filled with the noises that only forty-one "wanted" boys can make. And they're proving the truth of Brother Buck's motto, "No boy is all bad."

Missions

Service

Dr. Howard Hamlin was chief of the department of surgery at South Shore Hospital in Chicago, a professor of surgery at the University of Illinois School of Medicine, and medical director and vice president of an insurance company when he decided to go to Africa as a permanent missionary. He was then fifty-one and a grandfather. His call had grown out of a summer's visit to a Nazarene Hospital in Swaziland. Returning home he had told his wife, "It'll be nice to see the children again, but all we have to look forward to is going back to Chicago and making more money. The African people really need me."

Dr. Hamlin's decision made a big story in the Chicago papers. A Jewish surgeon friend read the story and telephoned him. "I always figured something was wrong with you, Howard," he said jokingly. "Why are you doing this?"

"For the same reason that one of your greatest forebears became a great missionary," Dr. Hamlin replied.

Christ is healing today directly through His followers who bear witness to His redemptive love over a hot operating room table somewhere in a mixed-up world.

Involvement

Service

A telephone company foreman, moved by the plight of children with emotionally rooted speech defects, did something about it.

The man, who was also a speech therapist, used his spare time to construct a large doll containing a two-way radio. He discovered that previously speechless youngsters would converse readily with the doll, which carried the therapist's voice from another room.

Getting out of ourselves and into the needs of others can unlock our own creativity — and light a few candles in a darkened world. "Always seek to do good to one another" (1 Thessalonians 5:15 RSV).

Involvement;
Social Reform

Service

"Sharing the world of a five-year-old on the lower East Side of Manhattan can be as exotic and mind-expanding as visiting the Taj-Mahal," says Marni Gislason, an airline stewardess.

Miss Gislason is a coordinator for the Community Action Program, a nation-wide group of nearly one thousand Pan American employees who volunteer in day-care centers, drug programs, hospitals, old age homes, and schools in many parts of the world.

"When we started the program," she explains, "we approached it from the point of view of what's in it for the girl herself.... We stress the idea of mutual sharing. I feel I have as much to gain from my involvement in the community as the community has to gain from my being there."

Sharing

On long rides with our children, we sometimes stop the car to buy fruit, candy, or gum, I toss the bag into the back seat and call out, "Here . . . split."

One day my wife and I had a heated argument. Later we lapsed into an uncomfortable silence. The children then stopped their conversation. Finally, Karen, our seven-year-old, reached over and gave my wife a kiss on the cheek. "Here," she said, "split with daddy."

Robert Rich

Sermon

Shock

The story is told of a certain pastor whose congregation tended toward sleep whenever he began to preach. One Sunday he came prepared with a great solution to this problem. When he went into the pulpit the first thing he said was, "I feel that I must confess to you as your pastor, that I have spent several of the best years of my life in the arms of another man's wife." Immediately, everyone in the church was shocked into wakefulness. There were no more sleepers. Everyone was hanging on his every word. Then, he added, "My mother!" The congregation had a good laugh, and he'd accomplished his purpose.

But it didn't work for another pastor who tried the same technique. The trouble was that he was one of those individuals who could never remember the punch line of a story. One Sunday when he began his sermon he saw half the congregation drifting off to sleep. He decided that now was the time to try the "shocker" on them. He began, "I feel I must confess to you as your pastor that I have spent several of the best years of my life in the arms of another man's wife." Then, he paused . . . frowned . . . gulped . . . and added, "But, for the life of me, I can't remember who she was."

Blindness

Sight

At the Indiana School for the Blind one afternoon, a little boy asked his teacher, "Is a storm coming up? I hear thunder."

Thinking he might be frightened, she answered, "Oh, I don't think it will be very bad."

"Will there be lightning?" he persisted.

She put her arms around him reassuringly, "Why do you ask?"

"Because that's the only thing I can see," he replied. "And it is beautiful."

Indianapolis News

Silence

During World War II some Quakers walked boldly into the Berlin Gestapo office of Reinhard Heydrich, Himmler's deputy chief. They implored the butcher Heydrich for permission to take persecuted Jews out of Germany. Heydrich listened stonily to the Quakers. Then he asked them to wait in an adjoining room for his reply. There the Quakers sat silently, prayerfully, and meditatively. Quite unknown to them the room in which they sat was wired. Their request would have been peremptorily refused had they spoken against the cruelties which were being perpetrated against the helpless Jews. Or, if they had spoken out against the man Heydrich . . . such a normal thing to do. Their prayerful silence was broken by the dramatic announcement: "Your request has been granted." The Quakers knew the thunderous power of silence.

Sin

Bollingbrook police are searching for $30,000 in municipal bonds . . . the price allegedly paid by a 36-year-old Oak Park man for the purchase of a 12-year-old girl as his intended bride.

Ronald Johnson, of the Will County suburb, said the stepfather and mother of the girl, Fred and Rita Flynn, cashed the bonds and went on a spending spree.

"They bought a new car, new furniture and draperies for their $40,000 home in Bollingbrook and paid off numerous debts," Chief of Police Johnson said. "They spent all but $220 of it."

Police identified the alleged buyer of the girl as Harold Miller, a teaching assistant in the speech and theater department of the University of Illinois' Chicago campus.

Johnson described Miller as being independently wealthy as a result of a trust fund established by his late father. The girl's 43-year-old stepfather told reporters she was a runaway.

However, Johnson said Flynn admitted under interrogation that he delivered the girl Saturday to Miller at the Holiday Inn in suburban Willowbrook. As part of the bargain, the chief said, Flynn was to fly to North Carolina this week and lie about the girl's age so she could get a marriage license. Girls 14 or older there may marry with parental consent, Johnson said.

Flynn, a salesman for a steel and copper distributing company, met Miller several months ago while moonlighting as a cab driver in Oak Park. The alleged sale was arranged after Miller said he would like to have a young girl as a wife. The father ascribed the alleged sale to "money problems."

The couple has been charged with child abandonment and conspiracy to abandon a child, both felonies. Efforts are underway to extradite Miller on a charge of conspiring to aid in child abandonment.

The Oregonian, Friday, March 23,1973

Sincerity

When the old Roman sculptors marred a statue with a slip of the chisel, some of them would fill the crack or chipped place with wax and try to sell the statue as unmarred. Honest sculptors refused to deceive the people thus. They stamped their statues with the Latin words *sine cera* meaning without wax. From these two words we derive our English word *sincere*. Christ was "without wax." "Never man spake like this man" (John 7:46 KJV). So, our speech must be salted with sincerity, integrity, impunity, and impeccability.

Speaking

A speaker was engaged by two different organizations in a certain city, one at noon and the other a dinner banquet. A few days later he found the following note from the president of one of the organizations:

"Dear Professor: I see that you have charged us $50 for giving a fifteen-minute talk at our banquet. I have since learned that you gave a similar talk before the Sinawik Club and charged them only $25. Will you please explain this discrimination?"

The professor promptly replied: "At the luncheon club I was the only speaker. At your banquet I was obliged to endure an hour and a half of acute mental distress while listening to speeches by you, the mayor, the chief of police, and a member of the state legislature."

Speaking

Artemus Ward, one of America's leading lecturers and platform personalities, used to tell a good story on himself. While vacationing in the deep South, he wanted to keep in practice, so he offered to give a series of lectures free before the inmates of the local prison. The offer was accepted by the authorities but his appearance was coolly received by the prisoners. He was left with the impression that they would rather have been left undisturbed.

Before Ward's second appearance in the series was due a delegation of inmates called upon the warden.

"We wish to protest against these lectures," said the spokesman. "They were not included in our sentences."

Speaking

A well-known actor was seated at the guest table at a dinner given in a New York hotel. Among other things he was known to be a free thinker along theological lines. When the hour for starting the dinner arrived, the toastmaster, a religious man, discovered there was no minister of the gospel present, despite the fact that several had been invited. In the emergency he turned to the actor and asked him to give the benediction.

The actor rose, lowered his head, and in the midst of a deep hush said fervently: "There being no clergy present, let us thank God!"

Marion D. Mosher

Speaking

Airplane pioneers Wilbur and Orville Wright, a shy pair, hated to make speeches. Once at a luncheon they were scheduled to address a group of inventors. The toastmaster called on Wilbur.

"There must be some mistake," stammered Wilbur. "Orville is the one who does the talking."

The toastmaster turned to Orville who stood up and said, "Wilbur just made the speech."

Speaking

The speaker bores you, gentlemen?
He's also boring me.
But praise him gently when he's through —
He comes to us for free!

Virginia Moore

Speaking

A fraternal organization once asked George Jessel to play a benefit, and since it was in Brooklyn, his home territory, he agreed.

A few days later someone phoned him and suggested that he might also be able to line up Eddie Cantor. George said he would try and soon thereafter was able to report Cantor's acceptance.

"Ah, that's fine," beamed the chairman of the program committee. "Now, just one thing more. If you can also get Bing Crosby, you won't have to come."

Stereotype

People outside the church develop some peculiar ideas about the institution, its sacraments, ordinances, beliefs, rubrics, and liturgies. They feed on barroom hearsay. "You have to speak in tongues to be a Pentecostalist." "Catholics believe Mary saves." "Presbyterians believe dancing is a sin." "Lutherans are anti-Mason." "Baptists think they are the only ones going to heaven." "Methodists won't drink in front of each other." "The Brethren demand footwashing." "You have to belong to the local country club to be an Episcopalian." "The Christian Church rushes you into the baptismal tank when you join." "All the churches are full of hypocrites and crooks." On and on it goes . . . and where it stops nobody knows.

Parents

Suffering

For a Youngstown, Ohio, mother, the painstaking experience of raising a mentally retarded child was "something very different from what we ever imagined or hoped it would be." She added, "These years have been fruitful. Our child took us out of our insulated world and opened many closed doors to our

193

hearts. We broke out of those walls and saw the need of other human beings. As a result of this, we became actively involved in social justice in the world around us."

Suffering — other people's as well as our own — can be redemptive if we turn it, with God's assistance, into something positive.

Suffering

How much can one person bear? "More" would be the answer of Carson McCullers, the novelist, who was described at her death as having "a vocation of pain."

"Much of her art," a critic related, "seemed to have flowed from her own tortured life."

Before she was twenty-nine, Mrs. McCullers had suffered three strokes which paralyzed her left side. Discouraged, she imagined she could never write again. But gradually, a page a day, she resumed her work.

The ever-present pain intensified in her later years. Her husband committed suicide, and illness left her a virtual cripple. In a rare mention of her troubles, she said: "Sometimes I think God got me mixed up with Job. But Job never cursed God, and neither have I. I carry on."

Suicide

Victims of suicides formerly tended to be overburdened, middle-aged businessmen, but in recent years the victims are more likely to be teen-agers.

This is the observation of Jack Price, chaplain of the Albuquerque police department.

At a national meeting of the International Conference of Police Chaplains, Price found that twenty fellow chaplains from the United States and Canada are facing an increasing number of youthful suicides.

"We actually had an eleven-year-old kill herself," said a chaplain from Rockford, Illinois.

Suicide has become the third highest cause of death among young people aged from fifteen to twenty-four.

Surrender

Dr. A. J. Cronin, in an autobiography he called *Adventure in Two Worlds*, relates that, after many years of strain and effort in his professional medical career, he found himself still spiritually empty. He became aware that something was missing in his life. He had forgotten God.

Here and there he could see glimmerings of the Christian life in others, including some of the devoted and dedicated medical practitioners with whom he worked. What Dr. Cronin finally found, the factor that revolutionized and redirected his life, he described in his own words.

"I have handed myself over to God, body and soul. It is this surrender, total, unquestioning, in complete and absolute humility, which is the true essential of belief."

God

Tangentialism

T

St. Jerome wrote to St. Paula encouraging her not to tempt Satan by taking a bath. The advice may have been superfluous, since most of the "virgins" were so unkempt as to be tempting to no one, Satan notwithstanding. One of these early saints was cited for his supreme holiness by the fact that lice dripped from his body as he walked to worship. The sheer filth in which the faith of that time was incubated must have kept many away from the nonantiseptic madness called Christianity.

One particular order of nuns for decades of tradition always wore their robes while bathing. Their reason: "The Great God can see through the bathroom walls." So to appear decent before Him at all times, they took baths fully robed. Did they never see the illogic in their visualization of a God whose miraculous vision could pierce walls but not robes?

Calvin Miller
A Thirst for Meaning

Kindness; Generosity

Teacher

The whole town buzzed with sympathy when a local social studies teacher was killed in an auto accident, leaving a widow with five children to support. The mother had been a teacher herself but had not taught in many years. A small collection was taken up by sympathetic friends and neighbors, but everyone knew it was not enough to support the family for very long.

Then, quietly Marie Ebbingham appeared on the scene. She phoned the principal for an appointment. To him Marie explained her simple solution to the family's problems. She was a certified teacher of social studies and proposed that she be allowed to finish out the dead father's contract year. She explained that she was now retired and living on her pension, and would not need the salary she would be earning. Therefore, she suggested that the school pay her salary to the bereaved family, until the mother could find employment for the following fall. Her solution was quickly and happily accepted.

Teacher

A teacher in Hillside, New Jersey, supplements his salary by operating a bulldozer during vacations. Not long ago he made an application for credit to purchase a home, stating that he was a teacher.

It was turned down.

The teacher resubmitted the application, this time putting down his occupation as a bulldozer operator.

The application was promptly approved.

From the *Hillside Times*

Teacher

The teacher I'll never forget is one I never had. But I never stopped searching for her. I began the search in Poland and continued it in France, Portugal, England, and the United States. In each of the twenty schools I attended I looked for her, but she was not there.

I knew what she would be like. She would love life; love and laugh at it at the same time. She would inhale air and exhale a private sort of joy that she would not mind sharing. Her face would be her own business; she would not have to be pretty by anyone's standards, especially not mine. But there would have to be a depth in her eyes, and within that depth I intended to sail to the lands of riches. Later, sailing alone, I would not be a stranger there, because of her.

She would not be perfect. I expected to get mad at her sometimes. I hoped we would like each other well enough to argue long after all the other kids had gone home. She would have some habit that I would love and remember her by: drumming her fingers on the desk, or blinking her eyes, or looking out the window when someone's recitation was a bore.

But she was never there. Never there to tell me my grades did not matter as much as what I learned. She was not there as I stood behind one blackboard after another because I had been "bad." She was not there to understand why it was I never spoke in class. She was never there to tell me that being different was not in itself bad.

She was not there for me. But she is for my daughter. The teacher we'll never forget is Sister Mary Magdalene of the School of the Holy Child in Suffern, New York. The first time I saw her I knew the teacher I never had did exist. The only thing was, the timing was wrong for me. But not for my daughter, thank God!

Grade Teacher

Teaching

Mingling in the crowd at a college reunion, two old grads ran across one of their former professors. "I don't suppose you remember us from our college days, but we remember you," one alumnus said.

"Yes, you taught us French or history or something," added the other.

"Isn't it a pity," observed the professor dryly, "that I never succeeded in making clear to you the difference."

Christ

Teaching

In her book *Some Are Born Great*, Adela Rogers St. John recalls: "Once, long after his presidency, I was talking with

Herbert Hoover and he spoke of Teaching, Teachers and the Teaching profession in words I've never forgotten. He was, perhaps, not everybody's ideal as President of the United States, but as an engineer he had no equal here. Graduated from Stanford, he had practiced his profession as a mining engineer in Australia and China as well as the United States, and finally in England became the chief consulting engineer of his time. Nobody seemed to build a dam or enter into any engineering development anywhere in the world without first coming to consult the former president.

" 'Speaking,' he said to me, 'not as a religious man, not even as a Christian — which I hope I am — the greatest Teacher who ever lived was Jesus. His teaching is brilliant, beautiful, persuasive — and above all, He taught anyone anywhere, by the roadside, on the mount, on the sands of the Sea of Galilee. They didn't have to have credentials or grades, they just had to have interest enough to stand still and listen. And His Teaching has come down to us, over centuries, as no other teaching has. Not too long ago the *New York Times* listed His Teaching from the Mount as the most important event in all history. He had something wonderful to say and He said it wonderfully and it still means more to us than anything else that ever happened.' "

Football; Speaking

Testimony

Clendon Thomas is everything but timid on the football field. Playing for the University of Oklahoma he topped all other major college scorers in the nation during his junior year. All-American on the University of Oklahoma squad that won forty-seven games in a row, he went on to play defensive back with the Pittsburgh Steelers.

Clendon is also a dedicated Christian, known for his high moral standards. Since his conversion at the age of twelve he has attended church and Sunday school regularly. Yet he says, "I was the shy type . . . the kind of kid who sat on the back pew and listened. Until I was a freshman in college," he adds, "I was afraid to give a devotion or speak. Then, a pastor persuaded me to speak at a Sunday school dinner. I thought it would be a small class of a dozen or so members. But when I got to the restaurant, I found a large group of adults, including the governor, waiting to hear me speak. I literally trembled as I stood up. I stumbled and stuttered through my talk. I must have mumbled a hundred uhs and ahs. But, afterward the governor thanked me for my sincerity. Well, I was sincere in my testimony for Christ, but I was also scared. Since then I have given my testimony many times, but I'd still rather face the toughest tackler in the league than speak in public."

Graffiti

Theology

Graffiti found on a wall of St. John's University:
Jesus said unto them: "Who do you say that I am?"
And they replied: "You are the eschatalogical manifestation of the ground of our being, the kerygma in which we find the ultimate meaning of our interpersonal relationships."
And Jesus said: "What?"

Tomorrow

When news reporter Marguerite Higgins was covering the Korean War, she received the Pulitzer Prize for her perceptive, sensitive stories. On one occasion she wrote of being with the Fifth Company of Marines. It was early evening and the company stopped the long march to have supper. The men were experiencing bone-deep fatigue, anxiety, fear, and death. One huge marine leaned against a tree as he ate his cold meal from a tin can. He had been in the field for many days and his clothes were stiff with dirt and cold. His heavily bearded face was encrusted with mud, and was almost expressionless because of the immense fatigue he was feeling. One correspondent in the small group of reporters who were on the scene, obviously trying to get an exciting lead for his next article, asked the marine a strange and perhaps insensitive question: "If I were God and could grant you anything you wished, what would you want most?"

The marine stood motionless for a few moments, giving the question deep thought. Then, he looked up at the reporter and said, "Just give me tomorrow."

Alcohol; Drugs

Tragedies

At the close of church service, as the minister was concluding his introduction of new members, my "beeper" went off. The operator asked me to call the hospital. I went into the pastor's study, telephoned the hospital, and learned that my senior resident wanted to report the new admissions, as well as some problem cases, to me. There were seven new admissions, three of them from overdosage. One young man had taken a handful of an antidepressant. A second girl, while under the influence of alcohol, ingested twelve tranquilizer tablets.

A third girl, fifteen years of age, was a known chronic alcoholic. Think of it — the daughter of a secretary for one of our thoracic surgeons. Her previous admissions included one to the state hospital, a transfer from our institution. Now she was back again, on the verge of delerium tremens from alcohol, and having taken large amounts of an antihistamine medication for sea and air sickness, and a decongestant for colds and hay fever.

A fourth admission was that of an older lady, name and age unknown, found in a coma on the streets of El Paso. Her spinal fluid was full of blood. A fifth admission came from the jail — an ill prisoner. The sixth was a diabetic in insulin shock from overdosage of insulin or not eating enough to cover the insulin she had administered. Finally, the last admission was a disturbed individual with convulsive seizures, possibly from drug withdrawal.

After discussing the management of each case, I hung up the phone and looked at the list I had made while talking to the resident. Then I prayed, "O God, what is happening to our nation, our people, our young people? Please bring revival and redemption to our nation, once founded on Christian principles, now indifferent to the Christian message, in despair, and locked in by drugs. Have mercy, O God, on America; we have wandered far from Thy kingdom."

Trouble

A small trouble is like a pebble. If one holds it close to his eyes, it fills the whole world and puts everything out of focus. If the pebble is held at a proper distance, it can be examined objectively for what it's worth. If a pebble is thrown on the ground, it is seen in its true setting — a tiny bump in one's path.

Understanding

Wes Parker, Los Angeles Dodger baseball player, was asked to do some emergency baby-sitting for a neighbor's six-month-old child when a familiar crisis arose. Wes frantically called a friend and asked, "How do you change a diaper?" "Place the diaper on a table like it was a baseball diamond with you at bat," his friend said. "Fold second base over home plate. Place the baby on the pitcher's mound. Then pin first and third to home plate." Wes understood perfectly.

Understanding

The *New York Times* ran a feature story about an experience of a young schoolteacher who thought she knew all there was to know about her sixth grade pupils, until the day she asked them to write little essays about themselves. When she read their papers, she was amazed to discover how little she did know about them.

One very shy eleven-year-old boy was a particular worry to her because she felt he was terribly insecure. His paper read as follows: "Leonardo DaVinci was a man like me. He had all kinds of ideas, but they didn't always work. So do I. He started lots of things he didn't finish. So do I. Some of his inventions are used today, like tanks. He was also good at art and many other things. So am I." Obviously the teacher found a self-confidence there she'd never seen before.

But there was another boy who, on the surface, was brash and brassy. He was the student who gave his teacher her "Excedrin headache" every day. But she was amazed to discover in his essay a little boy who was unsure of himself and very discouraged. He wrote: "I am a big tease. That's what everyone says, except my father, who says I'm a bully. Some-

U

times I tease people on purpose, but not always. Sometimes I can't seem to help it. Sometimes I tease my mother. I tell her I'll be ruler of the world in twenty years and my brother will be the first to go. I can always make her mad by saying this, but my mother should know that I'm not that kind of person."

That is a most poignant sentence. The one person who might really be expected to know him, the one he was counting on to know him, was his mother. And even she didn't know what kind of person he really was.

Graffiti

Upsmanship

Graffiti is a popular form of expression in today's society. A minister I know couldn't resist temptation as he walked past an empty wall. He wrote, "I pray for all." A lawyer came along and, seeing the minister's statement, was inspired to write under it, "I plead for all." Not to be outdone, the next passing doctor wrote, "I prescribe for all." A blue-collar worker stopped to read each statement carefully, then picked up the chalk and wrote: "And I pay for all."

Upsmanship

At a dinner of foreign ministers following the American Revolutionary War, the British ambassador gave this toast. "England — the sun, whose bright beams enlighten and fructify the remotest corners of the earth."

The French ambassador followed with: "France — the moon, whose mild, steady, and cheering rays are the delight of all nations, controlling them in the darkness, and making their dreariness beautiful."

Benjamin Franklin then rose and, with his usual dignity and simplicity said: "George Washington — the Joshua, who commanded the sun and moon to stand still, and they obeyed him."

Vision

A loaf of bread bounced from a basket as a baker's truck turned the corner too quickly. When the loaf hit the pavement, a crumb broke off and lay beside it.

Almost instantly, three sparrows made a swoop for the crumb. When the contest was over, two of the birds flew away without a bite, and the other one carried off a meager breakfast. The loaf was untouched, unnoticed.

The crumb was worthwhile as a pickup; it was nothing as a prize. Just a little wider range of vision, just a little more faith, and each bird would have been satisfied. How often our own eyes are blurred to our own opportunities while we fight for crumbs.

Arnold Healey

Water

A man who had served for many years in a large downtown parish decided to shift gears in his middle-age by settling down to pastor a small, rural congregation. This occurred many years ago, but let him tell the story of his first big, country meal in a parishioner's home:

"The eating was so good it was almost sinful: baked ham, fried chicken, roast beef; sweet potatoes, mashed potatoes; vegetable casseroles dripping with butter; fresh-baked bread and rolls; and for dessert . . . hot blueberry pie topped with home-made vanilla ice cream. But all through that wonderful meal something kept bothering me, and I just couldn't enjoy it.

All during dinner I kept hearing the obvious sound of running water, and it really bugged me. Back in the city that sound was bad news. It meant that someone had left a tap open and the sink or tub was about to overflow; or there was a leak in the plumbing and the ceiling was about to break loose. For two hours that sound of running water bothered me. However, since it was my first visit to the parishioner's house, I was reluctant to say anything. Finally, I could contain myself no longer. When I asked about it, the host smiled and explained it to me.

"It seems that forty years before, when the farmhouse was built, a spring of water was discovered right in the middle of the property. So they built a spring room around it, then designed the house around the spring room. For forty years the people who lived in the house had been refreshed and nourished by this spring of water welling up right in the center of their home."

Neighbors

Welcome

My summer neighbors might have pinned a note to my door: "Welcome back to the Adirondacks. We know it's hard for you to come back without your good husband to this beautiful spot where you shared your love of woods, hills, ponds, and birds. Let us know if there is any way we can help." At such a note I would have choked a bit, dialed the neighbor's number, and said thank you in a voice of determined cheerfulness.

There was no such note on my cottage door. Instead, an anonymous neighbor had been more perceptive. A chunk of fresh suet hung in the white birch tree nearest the center of my big picture window. A hairy woodpecker was busily eating at it while two red-breasted nuthatches waited their turn at the suet bag. For the three days the suet lasted — the three lonely first days that would have been hardest for me — a succession of birds ate outside my window, carrying the welcome of my neighbors with its message that love is stronger than death.

Mrs. Lincoln D. Kelsey

Wickedness

New industries develop special skills, and the concentration camp industry was no exception. Adept *sonderkommandos* (specialized details) learned to apply grappling hooks with skill to separate the bodies. Trained technicians learned to pry dead lips apart and deftly knock out gold-filled teeth. Talented barbers dexterously shaved the heads of dead women. Six days a week, the new elite worked in the concentration camps. On Sunday they rested, went to church with their wives and children, and after church talked with horror about the eastern front, where Russians were killing German soldiers, and commented on the barbarity of the Americans who were dropping bombs on German civilians.

At the Auschwitz concentration camp seven thousand Germans were thus employed. Here, seventeen tons of gold were collected from the teeth of the dead. The hair from the shaven heads was used in the manufacture of cloth and mattresses. The ashes of the bodies were used as fertilizer for German victory gardens. Fatty acids were salvaged for making inexpensive soap. According to a Danzig firm, this was a good formula: Take 12 pounds of human fat, 10 quarts of water, and 8 ounces to a pound of caustic soda; boil for two to three hours, then cool."

All these things were kept in strict secret until after the war when the truth was discovered. The Nuremberg trials disclosed

207

barbarous cruelty, sadistic medical experiments practiced on countless unfortunates whose only crime was their Jewish heritage.

God

Wisdom

G. K. Chesterton, the great Roman Catholic layman, was once asked by an interviewer what book he would like to have with him if he were marooned on a desert island. As Chesterton began to consider this, the reporter made suggestions: "The Bible? A volume of Shakespeare?"

But Chesterton shook his head. "No. I would like to have a manual on boatbuilding!"

His reasoning: With a manual on boatbuilding, Chesterton could leave the island and buy a hundred Bibles and reach countless men. God is more practical than any of us. He is always concerned about our predicament and our circumstances, and He always has a relevant word.

Bruce Larson
Setting Men Free

Witnessing

It is often true that that which is most upon our hearts will be most on our lips. In the case of the pretty senior at Arizona State University, her ultimate concern was her commitment to Jesus Christ.

As she reflected upon the Miss America pageant, Vonda Kay Van Dyke commented, "I was a Christian competing in a contest that some 'religious' people would criticize me for entering. But I wanted to be Miss America for one reason and one reason only. That was to have the opportunity to tell other people about the Christ I love and serve."

. . . She smiled as she recalled the tense moments that preceded her title selection. "I was sitting up there in the top five. I paused and prayed that something would come up in the questioning that would allow me to share my Christian faith with the millions watching television."

Then came Bert Parks' challenging query, "I understand that you always carry a Bible with you. Do you consider your Bible a good luck charm?"

"I do not consider my Bible a good luck charm, it is the most important book I own. My relationship to God is not a religion but a faith. I believe in Him, trust in Him and pray that even tonight His will might be done.

"I couldn't have asked for a better question!" she said later. "I prayed the Lord would help me in answering the question and He definitely did."

Josh McDowell
Evidence That Demands a Verdict

Conversion; Christianity

Witnessing

A few years ago in Thailand, a Fulbright scholarship was awarded to a bright young Buddhist from a remote, poverty-stricken village in northeastern Thailand. Had it not been for the scholarship, this boy would have ended his education in the sixth grade and today would probably have been tending water

209

buffalo. He was sent to the Prince Royal College, a church-sponsored boys' school in Chiengmai, Thailand, and for the first time in his life, had enough to eat.

One night shortly after he arrived at the Prince Royal School, friends found him crying. They asked him why. He told them it was because he had enough to eat while his family back home did not, and he felt bad because he had so much. His friends at the school, all Christians, passed the hat the next day and immediately sent a large sack of rice to the boy's family.

The boy was dumbfounded. How could these Christians care about his family? Why would they do anything for people they had never seen? What kind of strange persons were these Christians who were so concerned about him, a non-Christian? Why did they, who were also poor, sacrifice their scant savings to send rice? Why would anyone "feel" his heartache, and why would anyone care enough about him, a penniless farmer's son?

He was so moved by the witness of the Christians at Prince Royal School that he wanted to learn more about them. Eventually he decided he would commit his life to Jesus Christ. Today this brilliant scholar is the esteemed director of the Christian Student Center at Bangkok, and one of the dynamic young leaders in the Thai church. Those Christians at Chiengmai, Thailand, knew the meaning of the word *witness*.

Dying

Witnessing

One day during medical rounds at the Methodist Hospital, I paid my first visit to Mr. Roberts. Mr. Roberts, who weighed 280 pounds, had heart disease, had been an asthmatic for years, and now had cancer wrapped around his windpipe. Although he had led a self-centered, dissolute, dissipated life, he was fortunate in having a lovely Christian family who had prayed for him for many years.

As I walked into his room, I heard a minister presenting God's magnificent offer of salvation to Mr. Roberts. The old, old story was being told in a quiet, gracious, loving way. Not wanting to interrupt this spiritual counsel, I walked out intending to visit my other patients before returning. In the hospital corridor, certainly by divine direction, I felt compelled to return to that room immediately. Walking back into the room I asked the minister, "Will you please excuse me for just a minute?" (I knew the way things were going medically for Mr. Roberts and that he was close to death.) "Mr. Roberts, this man is offering you the most important gift of your life. Won't you listen to him? I want you to know that your doctor is a Christian, and that I have made this vital decision you're being asked to make. Won't you accept Christ?"

Ten days later Mr. Roberts died. Shortly after his death one of his sons came up to me, face shredded with emotion, tears running down his cheeks. I thought, *This fellow is really broken up over his father's death despite the fact that I had warned the family of the magnitude and hopelessness of his father's medical problems.* To my surprise he grabbed my hand saying, "Dr. Dennison, for thirty years we have prayed as a family for my dad to find Christ. And he found Him in this hospital through our pastor's and our doctor's faithfulness in telling a dying man of God's forgiving love in Christ."

Words

Candidate: In Latin *candidus* means "glittering," "white." In ancient Rome, a man campaigning for office wore a white toga and was consequently called "candidatus," "clothed in white." From this comes our word *candidate*, with the meaning of "one campaigning for office," but without the oral significance as to dress.

From the same Latin word *candidus* we have our adjective *candid*. This word was first used in English with its literal meaning "white," but it is now applied figuratively to a mental quality unclouded by dissimulation or bias.

Words

A romantic tale lies behind the phrase "sub rosa." According to ancient legend, the Greek god of silence, Harpocrates, stumbled upon Venus, the goddess of love, in the course of one of her amorous adventures.

Cupid, Venus' son, happened along at an opportune moment and, by making a gift of a rose to Harpocrates, bought his pledge of secrecy.

Since that time the rose has been the symbol of silence.

During the Renaissance and later during the reigns of the pre-Revolutionary kings of France, the rose was a favorite architectural motif and was often sculpted on ceilings of dining and drawing rooms where diplomats gathered.

The obvious implication was that matters discussed "under the rose" were to be held in confidence.

William Morris
in the *Chicago Daily News*

Words

Rx: The origin of the symbol Rx found in the upper left-hand corner of every prescription goes back 5000 years. The Egyptians used the magic eye of Horus as an amulet to guard them against disease and suffering. The eye has two tails hanging from the center, and centuries later it reappeared in a form resembling our numeral 4. Physicians scribbled it on their prescriptions to invoke the assistance of Jupiter. By slow transformation, the numeral changed into Rx.

Dr. T. R. VanDellen
in *Chicago Tribune*

Words

Curfew: In the middle ages peasants were required to cover or extinguish their fires at a fixed hour in the evening, announced by the ringing of a bell called the "cover-fire," French *couvre-feu*. The Norman French used the word in England, where it was adopted as *curfu* or *courfew*, modern *curfew*, meaning the hour and the signal for citizens to retire to their homes. The curfew is now usually a signal for children to leave the streets and go home.

Words

Turkey: When the first Spanish conquerors of Mexico brought the earliest turkeys into Europe (about 1530) Jewish merchants introduced them to Greece, then part of the Turkish Empire. Sharp-witted Greeks were quick to see a likeness to the new bird and their old lords. It strutted pompously; it was inflated with dignity; above all, it had a little red headpiece like the fez the Turks wore. So they called it a turkey.

London Sunday Express

213

Words

Tantalize: In Greek mythology, King Tantalus offended the gods and was punished in an extraordinary manner. He was placed in the midst of a lake whose waters reached his chin but receded whenever he tried to drink. Over his head hung branches laden with choice fruit, which also receded whenever he stretched out his hand to satisfy his hunger. Tantalus became the symbol of such teasing and his name is the root of our familiar verb *tantalize.*

Worry

Once Handel, the great composer, found himself in desperate straits, his right side paralyzed, his money gone, and his creditors threatening to have him sent to prison. But his suffering spurred him to the mightiest effort of his life. Writing feverishly almost without stopping, he composed *The Messiah* with its immortal Hallelujah chorus in twenty-four days.

If he had relaxed and forgotten his worries, the world would have been poorer and so would he.